How to Preach

Ken Down

Arc Press

Arc Press
66 Ffordd Pennant
Gallt Melyd
SIR DINBYCH LL19 8PE
Wales

Copyright © 2011 by Arc Press

ISBN-13: 978-1500531805
ISBN-10: 1500531804

Table of Contents

Introduction - Speaking for God

The work of the preacher is the most important in the world. It is his task and his privilege to speak on God's behalf, to say the words that God would wish to say were He present. As the apostle Paul says, "God has committed to us the message of reconciliation. We are, therefore, Christ's ambassadors, as though God were making His appeal through us. We implore you on Christ's behalf, 'Be reconciled to God.'" (2 Corinthians 5:19, 20)

It follows, therefore, that the one who preaches must always remember that he is representing God and must ensure that, in his dress, deportment, words and attitude, he properly presents his Master. The pulpit is no place for vanity, pride or self-display, a fact that some public speakers - I will not call them preachers – forget. I well remember a former minister, who had been defrocked for adultery, coming to me and begging to be allowed to preach in my church. I asked him whether he felt that, in view of his recent behaviour, he was a suitable person to speak to God's people. With an almost contemptuous gesture he exclaimed, "I'm not worried about them. I want to preach for myself, for my own self-esteem." Needless to say, he did not preach in my church!

I try to practice this awareness in my own life. It is my custom, whenever anyone compliments me on a sermon, to reply, "Praise God." It is not that I reject compliments or that I am unappreciative of them, but that I wish to remind both myself and my hearer that the words which moved them were not mine, but God's. This stems from an experience when I first left home to go to college and train for the ministry.

I was working in a publishing house in Warburton in Australia, earning money for college, and one weekend friends took me down to a camp meeting held in Melbourne. Christians from all over the state of Victoria came together for a week under canvas, enjoying the meetings to which the best speakers in Australia were invited. The adults' meetings were held in the main tent, a huge structure that could hold three or four thousand people. Similar but smaller tents accommodated the young people and the children.

I was only there for a single day, but as I strolled around the camp ground during the lunch break I spotted Pastor George Burnside, a very well-known and popular preacher and evangelist in Australia. (I remember once hearing him preach. His sermon closed far too soon for our liking but when the disappointed audience looked at their watches we discovered that he had spoken for nearly two hours!)

Pr Burnside was a friend of my father's and only a year or so previously had visited us in India, so I hastened to make myself known to him, purely for the pleasure of renewing our acquaintance. He remembered me and, much to my surprise, asked me to tell a mission story during the afternoon meeting in the youth tent, at which he was the guest speaker.

My parents were missionaries in India and during my teenage years I was sometimes invited to speak in public. I regarded such invitations as sacred commissions from the Lord, but I always found them nerve-racking affairs where I performed my part adequately, but no more. Now I was to be matched with a man whom I and many others regarded as Australia's foremost preacher, before an audience of nearly a thousand young people of my own age. It was solely through a sense of duty that I agreed to speak.

The trouble was that I had no idea what I should say. As the minutes passed my mind resolutely remained blank. As the time for the meeting approached I walked into the youth tent, sat down several rows from the front and quietly panicked. Life in India was, to me, so humdrum and ordinary that I could think of nothing that might interest the audience.

The meeting began and after the usual hymns and prayers Pastor Burnside stood up to preach - and what a sermon it was! His text was a passage in Psalms 74:20 which says "the dark places of the earth are full of the habitations of cruelty" and as he enlarged on his theme he held the audience spellbound so that the only sound was the gentle flapping of the canvas, stirred by the fitful breeze.

Still I couldn't think of what to say and as the moments passed and the time when I must surely be summoned drew nearer my hands were clammy with cold sweat and my mind raced with prayers to God to give me words to say. I had read of people who, through nervousness or lack of preparation, stood in front of an audience and opened and shut their mouths, but no sound came out, and I dreaded that such would be my fate.

"And now," Pastor Burnside declared in his ringing voice, "we have a young man all the way from India who will tell us of his experiences in that dark land."

I dared not disobey, for Pastor Burnside had already spotted where I was sitting. Trembling, I rose to my feet - and as I did so I knew what to say.

Some years before my mother had written a book (I think she called it *Little Mission Hospital*) that in the end was never published. One of the stories in it concerned a tragic double murder that took place near the Christian hospital in Ranchi when a young farmer became convinced that his mother was a witch, responsible for the various losses that had come upon him. He stabbed her to death and then, when his father tried to intervene, stabbed him as well. This was the story that the Lord presented to my mind.

Not only did He give me what to say, He also gave me how to say it. Eloquent words, perfectly matching Pastor Burnside's style but in no way a parody of it, just flowed from my lips and the stillness of the audience before was as nothing to the silence with which they hung upon my words - yet not mine, but the Lord's. When I finally finished and resumed my seat in the audience it took a moment or two for Pastor Burnside to regain his previous ascendancy over the congregation.

Fifteen years later, when we returned to Australia for a brief visit, a young man came up to me and reminded me of this incident, saying that he had never forgotten the story I told on the Melbourne camp ground. Praise God!

I regard that event as my anointing to the ministry. From that moment on - with one single exception which I will mention later - I have never felt nervous before an audience, whether large or small, for I know that what I speak, I speak for God and the responsibility for its success rests with Him. That is why, whenever I am complimented about a sermon, I always reply, "Praise God," for the work and the words are His.

This was not the only incident where God gave me the words to say, nor am I the only one ever to have experienced such a miracle. I remember on another occasion being invited by a friend to preach in his church while he was away on holiday. We travelled over there the day before and stayed in our friend's home and as I drove I mulled over what I would preach about. It was my intention to speak on a certain topic, a favourite of mine, on which I had spoken many times before and which I knew I could present quite well, yet somehow the subject just wouldn't "jell" in my mind.

About half an hour after we arrived at the friend's house the phone rang. It turned out to be the church elder, ringing to inform me that that week the church was celebrating Communion, a fact which my friend had forgotten to tell me. I thanked the elder and as I put the phone down I instantly knew what I would preach about. Half an hour in the study and I had the sermon notes written out and ready. The sermon went well and seemed to be well received.

When my friend returned from his holiday I naturally gave him a report of what I had done in his church during his absence, but when I mentioned the topic on which I had preached his eyes widened. "That was just what that church needed!" he exclaimed. "I dared not speak on that topic for fear of alienating half the church members, but you, as a visitor, could get away with it."

Do not think that such experiences are limited to the ordained clergy. My son, a lay-preacher, was down to preach in a church in Worcester and my wife and I happened to be visiting that weekend to celebrate one of the grandsons' birthdays. That morning I came down to find my son sitting at the kitchen table, Bible open before him, scribbling notes on a piece of paper while he ate his breakfast. I made some jocular remark about leaving one's sermon preparation to the last minute and he said No, he had prepared during the week and had a sermon all ready, but when he woke up that morning he felt strongly impressed that he should speak on a different subject.

We went to the church and shortly before the service started a visitor we had never seen before walked in. He was welcomed heartily and mentioned that he had come up from Kent (for those not familiar with British geography, that is about 150 miles and a good three hours driving away) to visit Worcester and had felt impressed to come and join our worship.

My son preached a good, workman-like sermon, perfectly adequate but nothing out of the ordinary. Afterwards, however, I saw him closeted with the visitor and later he reported that the man had come up to him, shaking and with tears in his eyes and said, "That sermon was meant for me!" I don't know the details of how or why it was particularly applicable to that man, but in some way it gave him a message that was just what he needed at that time.

Was it an accident that he happened to visit that church? Was it by chance that my son felt impressed to change the subject of his sermon? Why God did not use a preacher in Kent to deliver that message, I do not know. Perhaps the man might have suspected that a preacher in Kent had prior knowledge of his situation; perhaps my son had the presentation style that would appeal to the man or get the message across to him, but whatever the reason, I am sure that God was responsible for both the message and the audience.

No one need say that they cannot preach. The only question is whether God has called them to preach. If He has, then the responsibility is His. He will give the words to say, both the content and the manner of the sermon - and when He is graciously pleased to use us in this way, then we can truly say, "Praise God" when others express their appreciation.

The Purpose of Preaching

In Romans 10:14 Paul asks, concerning the heathen, "How can they call on the One they have not believed in? And how can they believe in the One of Whom they have not heard? And how can they hear without someone preaching to them?"

The **primary purpose** of preaching, then, is to proclaim Christ - or, to put it in everyday language, to introduce Christ to people. Every sermon should serve to reveal Jesus, His character, His requirements or His plans. This task has never been so important, since heathen times, as it is today. Whatever of Christianity people in our culture used to know has been largely forgotten. Apart from vague ideas of babies in mangers, most young people - and many older ones - know absolutely nothing about Jesus. Certainly they are ignorant of what His advent means to mankind.

But the preacher must do more than merely preach what we might term "gospel" sermons. There are dangers he must warn against, duties he must present, promises he must reveal. The **second purpose** of preaching is to instruct God's saints in the great truths of the Christian religion as revealed by God's word and encourage them to right living. The preacher must rebuke sin, expose error, exhort to righteousness, encourage the weary and comfort the sorrowful. The faithful minister must preach true doctrine in order that his hearers might be warned against false doctrine and the many "seducers" who abound in these last days.

The **third purpose** of preaching is to explain the word of God so that the people can understand it. The Bible has become remote from everyday life. Sowers and fishermen are outlandish curiosities in an age when food comes from supermarkets, milk from cartons and droughts are something that require government, rather than Divine, intervention. Despite the valiant efforts of Bible translators, the most popular Bible is still the *King James Version* with its old-fashioned language. Many church-going people feel that a few verses, recited without understanding like an incantation, constitute a living spiritual experience. The preacher must study so that he can "rightly divide" the word of God, correctly interpreting it with regard to its historical, geographical and literary context. He must be able to apply it to his hearers so that they will perceive it as the living word of God, speaking to them today.

In all this the preacher must beware of presenting his own, peculiar opinions as though they were infallible truth. The pulpit is no place in which to indulge in polemics against those of a different opinion, nor for putting forward contentious ideas. Most churches have less formal meetings for Bible study and discussion and these are the place in which to be controversial and provoking or even outlandish, but once someone enters the pulpit he must be cautious and conservative.

This, of course, raises the question of when the preacher should speak out against some error in belief or practice held by his hearers. The answer is that he must do so whenever God tells him to. The wise preacher and pastor leads the sheep and never seeks to drive them. If he has done his work properly then his congregation will be ready to follow and accept what the Lord has given him to say. If they reject him, then at least let him be sure that such persecution comes from what he preaches, not how he preaches, for even a rebuke can be given in love.

Above all, a preacher must never address the sins of an individual in his congregation, unless those sins are open and notorious and the sinner is past redemption. A rebuke is best delivered in private and face to face (and in fact that is what Jesus commands us to do). If the preacher does not have the courage to do that, then he must keep silent. People rightly feel resentful if they think that they are being "preached at".

My own grandfather left his church for this very reason. Here are my mother's recollections of the incident. A divisive break-away movement was very active in that part of Australia at the time.

> "The church company became divided and warfare was bitter. After all that he had suffered for the faith without failing or complaining, Pat Murphy now became the most cynical and bitter. He and Herbert found error after error in what they had previously believed was truth. They laughed and scoffed at what had seemed to be plain statements in the Bible. Two other families, one of whom had been members of the church for over forty years, joined in the spirit of derision. Unfortunately the resident minister was not the man for the crisis; had he been more tactful the outcome might have been different.

"He frequently preached sermons on the subjects of the controversy. One week he climaxed his address by saying, in effect, 'These are our good old doctrines and if you don't believe them, you shouldn't be here.'

"Perhaps it was meant kindly, but Pat Murphy's Irish blood rose. He disdained to shake the minister's hand at the door afterwards.

"'If you mean for us to get out, we'll get out,' he declared loudly.

"Loud, angry words filled the porch of the little house of God which had been built and maintained at such sacrifice. How the angels must have wept over the scene!" (Goldie Down, *God Plucked a Violet*)

Pat Murphy and his family never entered the church again. Herbert, my grandfather, and his family shortly after also left the church. Many years later my grandmother and her daughters returned, but my grandfather died without ever returning. One trembles to think of those lost because a pastor preached publicly what he should have said privately.

Jesus commands us to "feed the flock". Let us make sure that that is what we do.

Types of Sermons

Teachers at theological seminaries have divided sermons up into a vast variety of types and sub-types. There are, however, only four basic types into which all sermons can be divided.

The first is the **explanatory** sermon. Here the preacher takes a passage of Scripture and explains its meaning. This type can be subdivided into **exegetical** and **expository**. The exegetical sermon takes no more than a verse or two - or even just a single word! - and explains what the passage meant to those who heard it for the first time. In the expository sermon the passage may be longer, a whole chapter or even a whole book. The preacher explains the meaning for today of his chosen passage. In some cases the two meanings may be identical, but in others they may be very different. For example, an exegetical sermon on Psalm 22 will talk of David's sufferings whereas an expository sermon on the same passage will concentrate on the sufferings of the Messiah.

The second is the **doctrinal** sermon, where the preacher expounds a doctrine of the Bible. This can be given in the form of a lecture, where the preacher does all the talking, or a seminar, where he invites feed-back from his hearers, or even of a Bible study, where he invites his audience to look up and read the Bible verses on which his sermon is based. The doctrinal sermon can be a simple presentation in which the doctrine is explained and illustrated, or it can involve a proof-text style of demonstrating that the Bible teaches this and not that.

There is a great need for doctrinal sermons, for only as God's people understand true doctrine can they discern false doctrine and teaching. Many preachers shun doctrinal sermons, fearing that they may find themselves embroiled in controversy or even official disapproval. The first thing is to be sure that you understand what the true doctrine is, then you must preach it clearly as a faithful shepherd of the sheep, and finally you must be prepared to endure controversy and even persecution. The great reformers and preachers of the past did not stir God's people by preaching pretty-pretty sermons on John 3:16!

The third is the **devotional** where the preacher takes a passage or an incident and uses it to inspire his hearers to action, whether that is building a new church or repenting from their sins, or to encourage them in hope or love for God. All too many preachers choose the devotional sermon exclusively, which often degenerates into "a few nice little thoughts" loosely based on the Bible.

The devotional sermon should not be despised, however, for it can be a powerful tool to inspire and encourage God's people. Some years ago I was the pastor of a church where the building was in a very poor condition. One Sabbath I felt called to speak on Haggai 1:4 and the result surprised me. Immediately the members, who only numbered about twenty-four, were inspired to action. They began to give generously to the building fund, the ladies organised sales and sponsorships, and within three years there was a brand new church on that site. Praise God!

Finally there is the **story** type of sermon. Usually we think of a re-telling of some Biblical story in which the preacher uses the experience of the Bible character in order to highlight the emotions and actions he wishes his hearers to imitate. If the story focuses on a single individual this is a biographical sermon. You can, however, use a personal experience in an autobiographical sermon. Beware, however, of the type of autobiographical sermon where the speaker's previous disreputable past is made to seem glamorous and exciting, more so than his or her present staid, respectable life-style.

Under this heading also I would include the **parable** or **allegory** type of sermon. I strongly disapprove of this type of sermon. Jesus used parables as illustrations in his sermons, simple stories with which the hearers could immediately identify and so memorable that when the Gospels came to be written the parables were the things that best stuck in the minds of Matthew and John and were transmitted to Mark and Luke. Most allegory type sermons are far otherwise.

I well remember suffering through one such sermon, presented by a young preacher at Newbold college. Purple globular masses bounced around a grassy meadow pursued by strange bovine creatures with five legs. The bright green sun shone coldly as the globular masses carried out some strange course of behaviour whose details I have forgotten. All I can remember is that every detail had some deeply significant meaning which was expounded to us in the second half of the interminable sermon, though what that meaning was I have long since forgotten. None of us have ever encountered purple globular masses or five-legged cows, so apart from some tepid admiration for the young man's ingenuity, his sermon made very little impact and was quickly forgotten. I only remember it as an awful example of how not to preach!

If you must use the parable type, do as Jesus did. Base your parable on some aspect of daily life with which your hearers can immediately identify. If you choose your parable wisely the meaning will be so clear to your hearers that, once you have told the story, the rest of the sermon is almost redundant. Furthermore, from then on, when your hearers find themselves in that particular situation, it will recall your sermon to their minds, which is a splendid way to reinforce your message.

You should not be unduly worried if a sermon does not neatly fit into one of these four categories. Neither should you wake up in the morning and say, "I am going to preach an expository sermon today." Rather, discover what God wants you to say, prepare it to the best of your ability, and then preach it. Let those categorise it who will.

Sermon Notes

Every preacher has his own way of writing his sermon. Over the years I have collected examples of various styles. Pr Timothy, an excellent man (with a most beautiful daughter who was at college with me), always wrote his out in full, with a thick, green felt-tip pen. The pen was so thick that he only managed five or six lines per page, with the result that he went into the pulpit every week clutching what looked like the manuscript for *Gone with the Wind*.

Pr David Owen, a young minister of my own age, jotted down notes on 3"x5" cards, usually ending up with nine or ten which he casually shuffled from front to back as he worked his way through his sermon. Disaster struck, however, the day he dropped his cards as he walked up into the pulpit - and he had omitted to number them from one to ten!

Some ministers write their sermons out in full and then memorise it word for word, a feat which, frankly, leaves me awestruck! Others write multi-coloured notes with Bible verses in red, other quotations in blue, main points in green, subsidiary points in yellow and illustrations in gamboge. Some have neatly prepared manuscripts, bound with pink ribbon, while others are satisfied with a few words jotted down on the back of an envelope.

In short, there is no correct way to write out your sermon. You must experiment and discover the way that is best for you. Here, however, is a sample of how I prepare my notes (when I have any). This is a sermon on the second coming of Christ. Notice how just the headings of what I am going to say are put down, with main points at the extreme left, sub-headings set in to the right and sub-sub-headings even further in. I also underline Bible texts, just to make them stand out a bit. Usually my hand-written sermon notes fit on an A5 sheet of paper.

I do not claim that this is the only way of preparing notes nor even the best way, but it is the way I use and I present it as a format that you may find useful.

Sample Sermon - The Second Coming

Scripture Reading   Matthew 24:1-13

How will Jesus return?
     Acts 1:11 "in like manner"
     Visibly
     Bodily

When will Jesus return?
     Matthew 24:36 "No man knows"
There are signs
     1 Timothy 3:1-5 "perilous times"
          Compare this with the present world
     1 Peter 3:1-13 "willingly ignorant"
          Theory of evolution
     Daniel 12:4 "knowledge increased"
          Growth of knowledge today
Conclusion: Jesus is coming soon!

Why will Jesus return?
     Matthew 25:31   "separate sheep from goats"
     Jesus comes to judge the wicked
     Jesus comes to save the righteous

Appeal: In which group will we be?

The ideal, however, is to preach without notes. This is not as difficult as it might seem. Imagine that I were to ask you to tell me how you get to work each day. Immediately and without preparation you could launch into an account of the method you use and the route you follow. It would be a clear presentation, beginning at your home and ending at your place of work, and backed up by illustrations of the difficulties you have encountered en route. And it would all be given without notes!

Ask a woman to describe her wedding day or the birth of her first child; ask a man to tell you about his hobby or the last holiday he enjoyed. Even if the account is a little disjointed, given a few moments for reflection and to arrange events in order, virtually anyone could give an account of these things - without notes. In other words, if you know your subject and if it is meaningful to you, then you can preach without needing notes.

The main requirement is that your sermon should follow a route – a logical progression from point to point, from introduction to conclusion. If that "route" is clear to you it will be as easy to fix in your mind as the route from home to work, as easy to remember, even when standing in the pulpit, and as easy to deliver, even if there are interruptions from fractious children or passing ambulances.

The advantages of preaching without notes are many: you can maintain eye contact with your audience, your sermon is fresh and immediate, you are not constrained by what seemed appropriate last night but you can respond readily to the changing mood of your hearers.

Don't be ashamed if you cannot do without notes. It is a fact that most preachers like to have notes or even a manuscript available, just in case they forget what they were going to say. The greatest advantage of having something written down is that it enables the preacher to have a clear idea of where he is going and how he is getting there. A sermon that rambles from point to point, touching on one subject after another, leaves the audience confused. Both the preacher and his hearers must be able to say, at the conclusion, what the sermon was about - and sometimes that is not the same as what the preacher said his sermon was going to be about!

In preparing your sermon, then, the first and most important thing is to have it clear in your mind what you wish to accomplish by your sermon. Is it to explain the parable of the Good Samaritan? Is it to warn your congregation against the dangers of spiritism? Is it to make an appeal to the young people to come to Christ and be converted? Whatever the purpose of your sermon, it is a good idea to take a clean sheet of paper and write it down in a single, short sentence and then keep that propped in front of you as you continue with your sermon preparation.

In the case of the sermon outline I have given above, the subject is the Second Advent but the purpose is to warn the hearer that that event is near and that they must be ready for it.

Bible Helps

All that the aspiring preacher needs, really, is a Bible, for Bible truth is what he must preach. The sayings of men, however learned, are no substitute for a simple "Thus saith the Lord". Nevertheless, there are "tools" which can make the task of interpreting the Bible an easier one.

The first and most important is a good concordance. A concordance is a book of words, arranged in alphabetical order like a dictionary, but instead of each word being followed by its definition, it is followed by a list of all the verses in the Bible in which it occurs. We have all had the experience of a verse hovering on the edge of our minds, one that will beautifully sum up our point or provide just the proof we need for our assertion, but all we can recall are one or two words from it. A concordance will help us to locate that verse quickly.

Of course it takes a little skill to use a concordance effectively. Suppose you wanted to find the verse "For God so loved the world". Words such as "for", "so" and "the" would be of little help, being so common. Even "God" is rather too common a word to be of much help. Look up either "loved" or "world" and you will rapidly find the correct reference, particularly if you know that the verse is in the New Testament, or in the Gospels, or, best of all, somewhere in John.

The most popular concordance is, probably, *Cruden's Concordance*. It is available in a variety of sizes, costs and degrees of completeness. Therein lies its weakness: it is not complete. Only the chief and most significant usages of a word are listed, and sometimes in the most idiosyncratic manner. For example, if you wished to find all the verses that mention the "first day of the week" it would be no good for you to search under "first" or "day". You must look under "week", where a special sub-division lists occurrences of "first day of the w".

I can strongly recommend *Strong's Concordance*, which is an exhaustive one. (Both of these were made by indefatigable clergymen in the days before computers. One marvels at their patience!) Not only is every occurrence of a word listed by Strong, but every word is listed, including such unhelpful ones as "and", "the" and even "a". In addition, by an ingenious system of numbers, you are shown which Greek or Hebrew word is used in each verse. This is invaluable information, for both the expert and the beginner alike. *Strong's Concordance* is not cheap, but neither is it exorbitantly expensive and you should regard it as you would a tool for any other job. Quality is worth paying for.

If you have a computerised version of the Bible, you will have the facility for a word search that will do most, if not all that a concordance can do. Some packages even provide an indication of the Greek and Hebrew words in a way similar to Strong's. An excellent free computer Bible is the *e-Sword* package, a free download of the *King James Version* and many other versions (including foreign languages) but a small charge for copyrighted versions such as the *New International Version*.

Once you have found your verse, of course, you need to understand it. A commentary fulfils this need. There are two types, which I will call the **devotional** and the **informational**. Commentaries such as those by Dr William Barclay are the former; you could just about read a section from one of them and have an excellent sermon. These have their uses, but I always feel that when I want to get lessons out of a passage of Scripture, I will be a man and get my own - which may or may not be the same as the ones Dr Barclay gets. Indeed, there may be more than one lesson to be drawn from a passage of Scripture, but if I read Dr Barclay I will only see the lesson he sees and miss the lesson the Lord would have me discover.

Then there is the informational commentary which explains the meaning of words and gives you the historical or geographical back-ground to a verse. This is the only commentary I possess and the ten green-bound volumes take up a large amount of shelf space. I believe it is now available on disk for the computer. Ironically, when this commentary does attempt to give the theological meaning of a verse it is often debatable and sometimes just plain wrong. Even worse, when a verse is extremely difficult to understand, the commentary is often silent about it, a most annoying habit! Nevertheless I find it invaluable in helping me understand the Bible.

Many beginning preachers feel that they need to learn Greek and/or Hebrew in order to give of their best. Nothing could be further from the truth. This is not to say that a knowledge of these original languages is valueless, but only that modern translations give the meaning of God's word so plainly that only someone who is intimately acquainted with these languages is likely to better their renderings. Even where experts are concerned, I have only ever heard a handful of sermons where I have felt that knowledge of the original language has contributed something that could not have been discovered from the English.

For those who wish to enter the difficult waters of Greek and Hebrew, however, there are aids and short-cuts. I have already mentioned the helps in *Strong's Concordance*. There are various grammars and teach-yourself books available for both New Testament Greek (which is not the same as modern or classical Greek) and Old Testament Hebrew (which is not the same as modern Hebrew). Your first step should be to purchase a Greek New Testament or a Hebrew Old Testament. I can recommend the Greek New Testament produced by the *United Bible Societies* but if you are short of money you might like to consider the *Interlinear Greek New Testament* produced by the Jehovah's Witnesses, which is fine so long as you ignore the sectarian *New World Translation* in the opposite column!

Be wary, however, in your use of Greek and Hebrew. Imagine a Hungarian who has learned a smattering of English. Would you trust him to lecture you on the exact meaning of a certain word? Imagine the possibilities for making a fool of himself! Only experts in the languages have the right to be dogmatic about such matters.

Unless you enjoy acquiring new languages, therefore, I suggest that you concentrate on learning about the history and geography of the Middle East. *Lion* produce some excellent introductions to the Bible which you can buy from both secular and Christian book shops. There is even a CD-Rom version of the *Lion Bible Handbook*. If your budget is small it is surprising what you can find in second-hand or charity shops. Original source books, such as the *History of the Jews* by Josephus can provide valuable insights if you can steel yourself to plough through them!

In the old days you might have to invest a considerable sum of money to build up a library of source books, but these days there is a vast amount of material available on the internet. *Project Gutenberg*, for example, has a huge library of original source material which you can read and download for free. However, unless you are dealing with a known author - the works of Luther, for example, or the Barclay commentaries - be careful of material found on the internet. Some of it is very valuable but there is much that is nonsensical, wrong, just plain rubbish.

Finally, the greatest aid to a preacher is a sympathetic and informed imagination. Your audience will get far more from the book of Ruth if you can imagine yourself in her place, a defenceless widow in the harsh world of Bronze Age Palestine, a woman in a patriarchal society, a poor peasant at the mercy of a rich landlord. Or perhaps you would care to look at it from the point of view of Boaz, an elderly bachelor who suddenly falls for an exotic foreign woman, reluctant to upset the even tenor of his ways but irresistibly drawn to this intriguing girl.

These days, however, there is one other book that I could recommend: a good English grammar and dictionary. A preacher should strive to use the very best for his Master, and that includes the very best English. Like, a preacher who, like, uses slovenly and incorrect speech, like, ain't gonna impress nobody, man!

I have seen - and heard - preachers who took great care over their dress, wearing an expensive suite or ornate "preaching gown", who were most particular about their appearance and ensured that they were well or even expensively groomed, yet who went into the pulpit and dropped their 'h's, never pronounced the final consonant of words, and used garbled grammar and a jumble of words that obscured their meaning. Few people will remember what you look like, but everyone will remember what you sound like!

It may sound horribly conventional, but the preacher should endeavour to use "standard" English, both in sentence construction and in pronunciation. The only exception is where he knows that he will be speaking to an audience of his compatriots. I well recall one man who was interested in learning how to preach. Unfortunately he came from the Gorbals area of Glasgow and his accent, though probably quite intelligible to other residents of the Gorbals, was completely impossible to follow. Even I, who pride myself on being able to follow most accents, usually had to ask the poor man to repeat anything he said two or three times before I grasped his meaning. I had the difficult task of tactfully explaining that he couldn't even attempt to preach until he had overcome his accent - and at fifty-six that proved an impossible task. (Of course, if he had felt called to minister in the Gorbals, that would have been a different matter!)

Sermon Structure

Every sermon must have a beginning, a middle and an end. Teachers of homiletics call them the **Introduction**, the **Body** and the **Conclusion**. If we think of a sermon 25 minutes long, then the introduction should take 2-5 minutes and the conclusion 4-6 minutes. In other words, about the same length of time for each.

When you are preparing your sermon it is a good idea to begin with the end. You will already have written down the purpose of your sermon and the **Conclusion** is the place to express that purpose. It is good practice to sum up the reasoning of your Body and show how that leads to the conclusion you wish the congregation to reach. A memorable phrase or slogan that will ring in the people's ears as they leave the building is excellent, if it can be achieved. Another good way to end is by means of a story that sums up what you have been trying to say and points towards what you wish to accomplish.

The aim of the **Conclusion**, then, is to present your congregation with something memorable that they can take away with them as they leave the church.

Next consider the **Introduction**. This should be interesting and thought-provoking, it should pique the interest of your hearers so that they are eager to hear what you have to say next. Your introduction may be a story that highlights the problem you wish to address, it may be an explanation of a dilemma or a paradox that your sermon will solve, it may set forth a false belief that your sermon will put right. Be innovative in your introductions: a song, a picture drawn on the blackboard, a conjuring trick, something recorded from the radio or even the children's story, can all provide an arresting introduction on occasion.

The aim of the **Introduction** is to make your congregation eager to listen to the rest of your sermon.

Finally comes the main **Body** of the sermon. Although this is the part that will occupy you longest when you deliver the sermon, it is not the part that will be remembered longest or that will make the most vivid impression. Nevertheless, you must strive for logic and reason in the **Body**; point must follow point in a manner that your hearers will recognise as logical and compelling, so that they travel with you from the Introduction to the inescapable Conclusion.

It is interesting to listen to those who phone in to radio programmes. Some callers put their points clearly and concisely and are a delight to hear. Others are the very opposite: they ramble, they bring in lots of irrelevant details and their point, whatever it is, is lost in a forest of side issues. It is noticeable that it is this second sort of caller who is interrupted and cut-off by the presenter of the programme.

Professional script writers know that there are five methods or tricks that are key to an effective speech. These are:

Contrast This can take the form of an argument - "on the one hand this, on the other hand that" - or a short pithy catchphrase. Dr Des Ford was an expert in catchy contrasts. For example, one of his sermons revolved around "The Law of Love or the Love of Law", which not only summed up his message but has remained stuck in my mind for over forty years! One of John F. Kennedy's most famous speeches revolved around a contrast: "Ask not what your country can do for you; ask what you can do for your country."

Triplets The human mind seems programmed to grasp three ideas more easily than either two or four. A good sermon will have three heads - see below - and each head may be subdivided into threes again. If you can include a contrast in with the triplet, so much the better! For example, a sermon on the Fall might have these three heads: 1) Man is lost 2) God seeks 3) Man hides. Notice how the third point is a contrast with the first two.

Alliteration Alliteration is when all the words - or at least the most important ones - all begin with the same letter. Des Ford's "Law of Love or Love of Law" is alliterative. A somewhat artificial example might be, "Calvary Cancels Criminal Conduct". Alliteration is an aid to memory - both yours and that of your hearers!

Bold Imagery It has been truly said that a picture is worth a thousand words, and a word picture is worth almost as much. Don't be afraid to exaggerate if that will get your point across. No Middle Eastern farmer, sowing by hand, would be quite as inept as the sower who went forth to sow, nor would the yield in good ground be quite as abundant as Jesus described, but the story has stuck in people's minds for two thousand years.

Finally, **Know your audience**. A sermon which will galvanise one group of young people will fall totally flat with another group. A sermon that will have a group of young scientists on the edge of their seats will pass totally over the heads of a group of elderly farm workers. Get to know the people in your congregation and you can "angle" your sermons to appeal to them and to meet their needs.

When you have written your **Body** lay it aside for a day or two and then come back to it. Read it through carefully and consider every point. Does each point lead logically into the next? Is there anything that can be cut out without detracting from the line of reasoning and argument that you are following? Is there - occasionally - something that needs to be added?

Of course you may still be at the stage of wondering what on earth you are going to say for twenty minutes. Here is a tip that I have found invaluable. Robert Louis Stevenson wrote a little poem:

> I keep six honest serving men
> Who taught me all I knew,
> Their names are What and Why and When
> And How and Where and Who.

The aspiring preacher can find these same serving men very useful as he seeks to organise his thoughts. For example, here is how they might be used in an outline for a sermon on the Second Coming of Christ.

> *How will Christ return?*
>> *Bodily and visibly*
> *Why will Christ return?*
>> *To put an end to sin*
>> *To rescue the redeemed*
> *When will Christ return?*
>> *No one knows*
>> *Therefore we must be constantly ready.*

The remaining questions of Who, What and Where are, perhaps, less useful in this case, though with a slight change in the question even they can be used.

What will happen when Christ returns?
Who will be saved when Christ returns? (or Who will be lost?)
Where will the redeemed go when Christ returns?

though that third question, perhaps, belongs to a different sermon entirely!

Notice that the first short sermon outline, as well as the longer one I gave you in a previous chapter, have three points, enough to make a good sermon but not too many to be remembered. Most of the best sermons have three points or heads and four or five should be regarded as the maximum. For effect these points can be contrasting, as in:

The love of God
The wrath of God
The patience of God

or they can be logically arranged to have a cumulative effect:

Love leads to sacrifice
God's love for us leads to God's sacrifice for us
Our love for God leads to self-sacrifice for God

A very effective method of ensuring that your points stick in people's minds is to use alliteration, where the heads begin with the same letter or sound:

Hopelessness - man's condition without God
Hopefulness - man's condition with God
Hope achieved - man's condition through God

A seeming paradox or a catchy slogan can make a very effective head. Dr Des Ford built up his quite considerable reputation as a preacher by the memorability of his sermon heads. For example:

A Law of love leads to the love of Law
Jesus: mad-man or God-man, but never just good man

Finally, a revered old preacher from the backwoods of America summed up his success in the following sentence: "First ya tells 'em what ya gonna tell 'em, then ya tells 'em, then ya tells 'em what ya told 'em."

Repetition is the best means of ensuring that your congregation remembers what you said. Repeat your heads often. For example, in introducing the third point in the above sermon the preacher might say, "We have seen that without God, man's condition is one of hopelessness; with God, man's condition is one of hopefulness; but now we turn to hope achieved, man's condition through God."

Even in the Body of the sermon repetition is a most useful tool. A good vocabulary and ingenuity of expression are useful here, for, of course, unless one does it deliberately for effect, simply repeating the identical words becomes boring very rapidly. A preacher might introduce the first point in this way:

"Hopelessness: man's condition without God. Friends, the man who finds himself without God is a man who is without hope. He has nothing to look forward to because he has no God to look up to. Hopelessness, the most miserable condition to which a man can ever descend, is all that is left to the man who tries to live without God."

There are four sentences in this quotation and each one is merely a repetition of the first, though you might not realise it immediately. Each one reinforces the one before it, so that your hearers become convinced, even if only subconsciously, that the man without God is a man without hope. Be warned, however, that repetition on its own will never serve to persuade if logic and reason are lacking. It would be as well to go on to give good, solid reasons why the man without God is also without hope.

Sermon Illustrations

This is such an important subject that I feel it deserves the dignity of a separate chapter. The purpose of a sermon illustration is to illustrate, to produce in your hearers that mental picture that is worth a thousand words. The most usual illustration is a story, but other forms can be a practical demonstration, an actual picture, a drama, a song or a personal testimony, either by the preacher or by a member of the congregation. Let us first consider the story.

The most important thing is that the story should be one to which your hearers can relate. It should be a story from their daily lives so that they can identify with the characters and the situation. A story about computers will be lost on an congregation of little old ladies while a story about sheep and shepherds may have little or no relevance to an audience of yuppies. To His audiences in first-century Palestine Jesus spoke of sheep, sowers and fishermen. Today we should speak about supermarkets, traffic jams and tax demands.

Above all, avoid like the plague those appalling collections of moral tales usually presented under such titles as *501 Sermon Illustrations*. The stories, which are usually wholly unbelievable, are almost always of the tear-jerker variety, sickeningly sentimental and so piously moral that they set one's teeth on edge.

The best illustration is one that begins "Yesterday, when I was down town, I ..." or "We have all been in a queue and ..." The only caution I would give is to beware of constantly drawing on your own family for illustrations. Not only will your children become exceedingly embarrassed at having their follies and foibles given public exposure, but your congregation will become thoroughly tired of hearing about your precocious offspring. Also, unless the illustration presents your victim in a favourable or even flattering light, never refer to someone in your congregation or known to them. Not every one can take a joke against themselves.

Then there are visual illustrations, which can take the form of pictures or diagram, either prepared in advance or drawn during the course of your sermon. Few of us are gifted enough to produce a recognisable picture as we preach – though I have heard of a talented man who could draw on a blackboard and leave everyone guessing until the final moment of his sermon when he drew one last line and suddenly you realised that it was a picture of an animal or a sunset or something.

Most of us can manage to write words or phrases, or draw arrows between words or circles around them. You need not be a Leonardo da Vinci in order to produce acceptable sermon illustrations. I have one sermon in which I review the laws of God from Eden to Sinai to Calvary and down to the Second Coming. Eden is represented by a squiggly circle on a stick – a tree from the Garden. Sinai is a sort of triangle with a rounded top for Mt Sinai. The only picture that is immediately recognisable is Calvary – a cross! Underneath these symbols I draw lines and write words. It's all very crude, but it is an effective visual aid that makes the subject understandable and memorable.

A black or white board or a flipchart are very useful aids, as is an overhead projector if you are at that stage of technology. These days in most Western countries a computer and video projector - about which I will say more in another chapter - are frequently used. A diagram, built up step by step, can often provide a wonderful means of clarifying the points you wish to make. Recently someone commented that they could still remember every detail of a sermon I had preached on the Millennium. They were from a church I had only ever visited twice - twenty-two years previously! I looked up my diary and discovered that what had made the sermon so memorable was the diagram I drew on the blackboard as my sermon progressed.

Using a blackboard or flipchart is not as easy as it might look. You must remember to write large, so that those furthest away can read. It is all too easy to start a line in large, bold letters, but then trail away into normal handwriting by the end of the line! Above all, your writing must be legible. If it is not - and using all upper case letters can help - you will need to use some other means or get someone else to write for you.

Another form of illustration can take the form of an interruption to the sermon: you can get someone to give a personal testimony relevant to your subject, invite people up on the platform to attempt a puzzle or answer a quiz. A personal testimony by someone who has found new life in Christ or victory over some particular problem can be a very effective and moving illustration. Beware, however, of those who dramatise the iniquity of their past lives: sin can be made to sound so exciting and attractive that the contrast with the present seemingly dull Christian life can have the opposite effect on young listeners to that intended, however much the witness may enjoy his new-found peace.

There are some who make quite a good living going from church to church to tell the story of their conversion. Unfortunately I suspect that much of this is an ego trip rather than a humble testimony to the greatness and goodness of the Lord.

There are various books of religious dramas available in the Christian book shops and, provided you have some keen amateur actors in your church, they can form an interesting introduction to your sermon or an unusual illustration during the course of it. If you can't find exactly what you want, try writing your own. Dialogue is not as difficult as you might think.

Chemistry teachers are past masters at the practical sermon illustration, but you don't have to know chemistry to use this method. A sermon on habit can be illustrated by hammering a nail (or getting one of the children in the congregation to do so) into a piece of wood, then pulling the nail out. Now try to pull out the hole! A sermon on grace can be illustrated by offering a free gift - 10p for example - to every child. I did this once, and the illustration was turned on its head when the golden-haired tot came up the front but stubbornly refused to hold out her hands and accept my free gift!

(Professional actors are warned never to work with animals or children, precisely because they are unpredictable, but so long as you are confident enough you can turn even the unpredictable to your advantage and your congregation will not hold it against you if the cute child behaves in a way you didn't expect.)

Not all of us have the gift of song but there may well be those in the congregation who do. If not, you can do wonders with a portable cassette recorder or CD-player. Again beware of excessive sentimentality in your choice of song.

Here is a sample illustration to a sermon on Salvation.

"Some years ago when I was just a young minister, struggling to make ends meet on my salary, my father wanted to help me. He arranged for a local bookshop to send me a quite expensive book that he had found very useful in his ministry and let me know that he was going to pay for it. Well, the book finally arrived; big, heavy, lots of glossy colour pictures, every page spoke of how expensive a book it was. I found it very interesting and was most grateful to my father for his generosity.

"You can imagine my shock when, several weeks later, I received a red letter in the post: the book shop sending me a final demand for payment and threatening all sorts of terrible things if I didn't pay up promptly. To my horror I discovered that the book was worth nearly a week's salary - and I had already underlined it and made notes in the margin, so I couldn't hope to take it back to the shop. I had quite a sleepless night, worrying how I was ever going to pay for the book!

"In the morning I went down to the book shop with the bill in my hand and asked to see the manager. I explained that I had thought the book was a gift and that I couldn't possibly pay cash for it, so could I please pay it off over the next couple of months? The manager frowned and my heart sank, but then he called in the person who handled the money and after a bit of paper shuffling they discovered that, in fact, the bill had been paid in full and that they had made a mistake in sending me the final demand.

"Can you imagine how I felt? Can you imagine my relief?

"We are in a similar situation. We owe a debt of obedience to the Law of God, a debt that we can never pay, not in a million years. God frowns at us and turns slowly to His books of record and there He finds a simple note: 'Paid in full two thousand years ago, on Calvary.'"

Now this whole story is a complete invention. To me, that is neither here nor there: we can all identify with being faced with bills that we cannot pay, with struggling to make ends meet on an inadequate salary.

We can all imagine the strain of facing a creditor and the relief to discover that we don't owe anything after all. I do not think that every one of Jesus' parables was factually true - the story of the Rich Man and Lazarus quite patently isn't - but if you have scruples about such things you can always introduce a made-up illustration with the words "Imagine if …

Scripture tells us that Jesus never spoke without using a parable - or possibly even never spoke except to tell a parable. To the multitude He was simply a storyteller, funny, relevant, entertaining, unforgettable. What was good enough for Jesus is good enough for me and should be good enough for you. Make your stories unforgettable and the morals will take care of themselves.

Delivery

No matter how well you have written and prepared your sermon, if it cannot be heard or is delivered in so boring a manner that your hearers lose interest, then you have wasted your time.

The first thing is to ensure that you can be heard. Try this experiment: sit or stand up, face forward, hold your head up straight and open your mouth wide. You have just provided a clear pathway for the air coming from your lungs. Any sound that the air carries with it will be clearly heard. Notice how the cavity of your mouth forms a sort of megaphone to channel the sound from your voice box towards the outer world.

Now lower your head so that your chin nearly touches your chest. Not only is any sound you produce now directed downwards but you have, as it were, put a kink in the pipe formed by your lungs, throat and mouth. If you try speaking your voice will inevitably have a strangled tone to it. Raise your head again but this time clench your jaw. No matter how loudly you speak, the sound is lost behind the impenetrable barrier of your teeth.

In other words, if you wish to be heard you must have a good, upright posture, you must hold your head up and you must open your mouth. It is amazing how many people get through daily life speaking with clenched teeth! On the other hand, look at an old movie of famous orators like Hitler, Mussolini or Indonesia's President Sukarno. They look directly at their audience with a bold, upright pose, and their mouths open so wide that it almost looks as though they are pulling funny faces at the camera. Whatever their morals, these were men who knew how to speak!

You must also breathe deeply and freely. Again, most people breathe using only the upper third of their lungs. Their shallow breaths are drawn in mainly by the action of the intercostal muscles between their ribs. Yet at the base of the rib cage is the strong diaphragm muscle, which acts like the piston in a pump to draw in large quantities of air. Put your shoulders back and use this muscle to draw in a great, deep breath. Your tummy will bulge as your diaphragm goes down, so don't try it if you are a woman wearing corsets - or a man whose trousers are too tight for comfort! (The cure, of course, is not to abandon proper breathing, but let out your trousers and take off your corsets.)

At one time my father had a number of young college students working with him. They were graduates from the ministerial course and it was my father's task to turn them into evangelists. Every morning the young men spent an hour or so under my father's tutelage learning the techniques of evangelism. With a blackboard and chalk he instructed them in the intricacies of electrical circuits, showing them how to wire up switches and light bulbs, how to calculate the number of 8 ohm speakers an amplifier could drive, and how to construct a primitive dimmer switch – all essential knowledge for the time. They were shown how to lay out an attractive handbill or newspaper advertisement and admitted to the mysteries of type faces and sizes, column inches and copy deadlines. They were given hands-on experience of carpentry, how to make a pulpit or build a font. They painted lettering on posters and banners, they stretched cheese-cloth on wooden frames and ran off screen-printed handbills using house paint and home-made squeegees.

In addition the young men were taught how to give a Bible study, how to capitalise on an opening, how to construct a sermon and, above all, how to preach. I can remember my father exhorting one unfortunate to breathe using his diaphragm, not his ribs. I can also remember the sheer terror in the man's eyes when, dissatisfied with the effect of his verbal instructions, my father left the room abruptly and returned with a leather belt. My father appeared not to notice the poor fellow's cringing, but strode up to him and cinched the belt up tight around his ribs, crushing them into immobility. With eyes popping and his face going slowly black, the hapless student was ordered to recite the Ten Commandments or the Three Angels' Messages until suddenly the penny dropped and he began to breath in the right way. (It is doubtful whether such high-handed methods would pass muster in these less enlightened days!)

Once you have the technique of breathing, it should be possible for you to take in a deep breath and talk at full volume for twenty seconds without having to stop and gasp for air half-way!

Of course it is easy to say such words as "how now brown cow" with a good open mouth. Less easy is "hitting horrible banditry in a pinch". Nevertheless, with practice one can improve one's audibility so that eventually even a whisper can be heard at the back of the church - a genuine stage whisper!

Once the volume has been produced, the next requirement is clarity. If you are going to be understood by everyone in the building, every consonant and syllable must be given its proper value. If a word ends with "t" or "d" that consonant must be sounded. There is all the difference in the world between

> *He looked and said to them*

and

> *'e looke' an' sai' t'em*

yet you would be surprised how many people, without thinking, produce the second rather than the first.

Always remember that language is your tool. You would think very little of a carpenter who left his saw out to go rusty in the rain, who used his chisels for screwdrivers and tried to smooth wood with a plane whose blade was chipped and blunt. Words are your chisels and hammers. Take good care of them. Learn how they are pronounced and used according to the best practice of the culture in which you find yourself. Don't be afraid to be thought "above" your congregation - you expect an ambassador to be "above" the ordinary person!

When I learned Welsh the teacher wanted us to learn what she called "colloquial" Welsh, which I quickly discovered was bringing us down to the level of the commonest of common people, with slang terms equivalent to "ain't" and "'orrible" in English. Because I intended to preach in Welsh rather than just chat in a pub, I refused to succumb and insisted on speaking Welsh that was grammatically and syntactically correct. Even though I know that my Welsh is far from perfect, I have been complimented many times on the "beautiful" Welsh I speak and the "mastery" I have of the language - simply because I use it correctly.

A while ago I had the privilege of preaching before a congregation that included Y Parch Gwilym R. Tilsley, a former archdruid of Wales. At the conclusion he shook my hand and told me, "Mae'ch Cymraeg yn gloywi" - "Your Welsh glows" - a kind compliment that made all my efforts worthwhile.

There is no reason why we cannot do the same with our native language and make our words "glow". The preacher who stands before an intelligent congregation and talks about "ten gween bo"les 'anging on the wall", who says "fink" for "think" and declares that he must draw his sermon to a close because "there ain't no more time" has only himself to blame if his congregation dismisses him as an ignorant sloven whose message can be disregarded.

Beware of adopting the peculiarities of speech you sometimes hear used by politicians on the radio. One ignorant ass says "refute" instead of "reject" and because he is "somebody", before you know where you are dozens of politicians and trades-union leaders are aping the idiot.

Likewise shun slang phrases. Still green in my memory is the highly placed minster asked by the happy couple to marry them in my church. In an attempt to be more impressive, this man had memorised the wedding vows but at the crucial moment his memory failed him. "If any man knows of any reason why these two should not be joined in holy matrimony let him speak now..." and there he stuck. I tried mouthing the words "...or forever hold his peace" but he didn't see me. Finally inspiration struck; he took a deep breath and in ringing tones declared, "If any man knows of any reason why these two should not be joined in holy matrimony, let him speak now or forever shut him mouf."

Your voice is produced by folds of skin in your throat vibrating together very rapidly. If your voice were pitched to the A-string of a correctly tuned violin, those folds would be knocking and rubbing together 440 times every second. That mounts up to a lot of wear over 25 minutes of continuous (and loud) speech! No wonder many who preach find that they have constant trouble with their voice.

The first thing to do is to make sure that your voice box is well lubricated. Your body needs six to eight glasses of water every day: make sure that it gets them. In particular take a glass of water immediately before stepping up on the platform. Nervousness may well make your mouth feel dry, a moist mouth can dramatically help you to cope with nervousness.

Beware of throat pastilles or drinks that contain drugs or sugar. These might produce a temporary easing of the symptoms of a dry or painful throat, but in the long term they cannot supply the one thing that is needful: water. If your body is well watered, you can rely on it to produce the correct amount of saliva, of just the right consistency to ease your vocal chords.

Secondly, deliberately try to lower your voice to a deeper pitch. People with hearing problems usually lose the higher frequencies first, so you will help them to hear you. A deeper voice is perceived as more authoritative and trustworthy, so you make your message more acceptable. Finally, even if you can only knock ten cycles per second off your pitch, that is 600 per minute and 15,000 in the course of your sermon. It might make all the difference between succeeding or failing to give the benediction in a good, firm voice!

This advice is particularly important for women, whose voices are naturally higher than a man's. In particular, women have a tendency, when they attempt to speak loudly, to become shrill rather than impressive. It is most interesting to listen to a recording of Margaret Thatcher before she became prime minister, and then compare it with one of her when she was at the height of her power. Her voice has become deeper, more controlled and more forceful.

Whatever your sex, avoid nervous giggles and over-much throat-clearing.

I remember my very first sermon, which was in Reading, Berkshire. I was overcome at standing in the sacred pulpit and that made me so nervous that my knees were trembling all the way through the sermon. What was worse was that my voice was a whole tone higher than normal and, try as I might, I could not bring it down! Fortunately I have never been that badly affected since.

As well as being audible and understandable, you should also strive to be an attractive speaker. There is nothing more deadly than a monotonous drone; those who are not put to sleep will definitely be alienated from you and, as a result, from your message. You should seek to vary the pitch, tone, speed and volume of your speech in order to emphasise the important points in your message. This is something that all of us do naturally in the course of everyday conversation, but very few of us manage once we are up behind a pulpit.

First of all, there are variations in pitch. Imagine that you are a policeman bringing bad news to someone. In a deep, warm voice, say, "Your son is dead." Now imagine that you are the horrified mother reacting to this news. In a high, shocked voice say, "My son is dead?"

However, be aware of the situation. If you are recording something for a tape or a broadcast, try to be a little extreme in your variations of pitch, as recording tends to deaden the voice. Avoid such extremes if you are before a live audience, because audiences tend to be sceptical about someone who varies pitch too much; it "sounds artificial" and "like people are trying too hard", according to a *University of Michigan* study.

Now for variations in tone. Imagine you are a patient adult speaking to your poor, senile father. "Don't do that." Now you are an impatient, exasperated parent rebuking a disobedient five-year old. "Don't do that!" Did you manage to get a certain weariness into your voice the first time and a sharpness the second time?

Then there are variations in speed. Imagine that you are giving directions over the phone to a Frenchman whose English is very poor. "Come - up - the - hill - and - turn - left." Now imagine that you are speaking from a blazing room with the fire between you and the door and giving directions to the fire brigade. "Comeupthehillandturnleft".

Actually, speaking slowly is much more difficult than you might think. Most people, asked to speak slowly, simply put longer pauses between the words but the words themselves are uttered in the same, rapid, way as before. We have to learn to speak the words themselves slowly, something like this: "Cuuummm uuup ththeee hiillll aannd tuurnn llleeffft". You might like to think of it as singing the words. Once mastered, there is something very satisfying in filling a room with resonant sound as you utter each word slowly and distinctly.

This is known as "declaiming" and it is an art worth practising. Pick a speech by some famous author or speaker – Shakespeare's "Friends, Romans, Countrymen, lend me your ears", or Martin Luther King's "I Have a Dream" speech, for example. Read it through aloud and time yourself. Then read it through again and see if you can stretch it out to double the length, but without leaving long silences between words or sentences. Record yourself on tape or computer and listen to yourself. Does the long version sound impressive or comical? Aim for impressiveness.

Don't be embarrassed if you find yourself pausing from time to time to gather your thoughts. Obviously you don't want it to become a mannerism, but the same *University of Michigan* study found that people who pause - around four or five times a minute - are more persuasive than people who are completely fluent and sound as though they are reading from a script.

Jose Benki, who led the *University of Michigan* Institute of Social Research study, found that the optimum speed is around 3.5 words a second or 200 words a minute. People who spoke faster than that aroused suspicion that they were trying to con their listeners, while those who spoke slower were seen as "not too bright" and "overly pedantic".

Finally there are variations in volume. A whisper can emphasise your point as effectively - and sometimes even more effectively - than a shout. Actually, a stage whisper isn't a true whisper, but rather a way of speaking your words with a certain breathiness while the volume hardly drops at all. Imagine you are a newspaper vendor, shouting "Read all about it!". Now imagine that you are an exasperated doctor, advising a patient to read the details of his medication; shouting would be inappropriate, but a quiet, emphatic voice makes the point just as well.

A word about prayer: when we stand in the pulpit to deliver the morning prayer there is nothing worse than the person who buries his face in his - or more commonly, her - hands, drops his voice to a confidential whisper and engages in a lengthy conversation with God. All the congregation can hear is a low murmur until the eagerly awaited "Amen".

Prayer from the pulpit is congregational prayer: you are taking the prayers of the congregation and making them audible. Use the same head posture and volume as when you are preaching - upright, open mouth, loud enough to be heard by the deaf sister in the back row. How can the congregation say "Amen" if they have no idea what you have been saying?

Gesture

However impressive your words, there is a silent language that can contradict them and even render them null and void - the language of gesture. This is such an important language that for your first sermon you will probably be better off to simply clutch the sides of the pulpit and stand rigidly still!

I remember our homiletics class at Newbold, in the course of which we each had to deliver a short fifteen minute sermon - with the others judging us! Some of the comments they made were merciless. One of the students was an extremely nervous young man who was appallingly self-conscious. I helped him prepare his sermon and listened to him deliver it several times over until he was word-perfect.

On the appointed day he stood in front of the class, his knees knocking, and nervously launched into his sermon. After half a dozen sentences, when he realised that he wasn't going to forget his speech or burst into uncontrollable stuttering, he began to relax and the quaver left his voice. About half-way through he had relaxed so far that he even let go of the lectern and his arms moved naturally, gesturing to emphasise his points.

Suddenly, out of the corner of his eye, he caught sight of something fluttering up above his head. He glanced up and saw that it was his own right hand. He stopped abruptly, visibly shocked, and, his face turning red, slowly brought his hand down, placed it on the edge of the lectern, folded his fingers into an iron grip - and then tried to carry on with his sermon! The rest of his time was a disaster as he stuttered and stumbled his way to an uncertain and unconvincing conclusion.

Once you are confident that you are not going to run out of things to say and that the audience is not going to eat you, you can start to loosen your grip on the pulpit and let your hands illustrate your words as you tell the congregation "Jonah's whale was *this* big" or "Zaccheus was *that* small". Most gestures will come to you naturally, just as they do when you are talking to a friend.

Try, however, to be aware of the gestures you are making and do not use the same stock movement of your hands whatever you are saying. Nothing can be quite so annoying to the listener as repetitive and meaningless gestures. The man who emphasises the occasional point by wagging his finger or pounding the desk is one thing. Quite another is the speaker who constantly wags his finger or thumps the desk in time with his words - all his words!

Watch people speaking on the television. Reporters, trade union leaders and politicians frequently fall into the habit of making a particular gesture over and over again until it passes from meaningless into positively irritating. (Some singers have the same fault!) It is so easy to fall into the habit of making a particular gesture whatever you are saying that the golden rule must be, unless your gesture is unavoidable, keep your hands firmly gripping the side of the pulpit. Shove them in your pockets, if necessary, rather than wave them around meaninglessly.

Remember, however, that gestures involve more than just your hands. There was a young preacher in Australia who tried to persuade his church board to spend several thousand dollars on a glass pulpit "so that the audience can see my body language". He was quite upset when the board felt it could do without his body language if the cost was going to be that high! (What I can't work out is, if his body language was so important, why didn't he come out from behind the pulpit?)

We do not have to be quite so stupid in order to use body language. Stand up stiffly straight to emphasise a point, lean forward over the pulpit to invite the audience to listen to an important secret, lean back to laugh at a joke, turn sideways to talk in the third person. Mind you, posture in general is important: never slump in the pulpit unless you want to give your audience the impression that it is all a bore – they might believe you!

Wherever possible, I prefer to come down from the pulpit and stand on the floor in the body of the church. I can move around, gesture and gesticulate, and there is nothing between me and the congregation. I have my Bible in my hands and that is all I need. However the churches where I speak are usually fairly small and most do not even have a microphone, so that sort of intimacy is possible. In a larger church you will need the height given by a platform so that everyone can see you and if there is a microphone on a stand, you may well be anchored behind a pulpit.

Unless you are speaking before an audience of thousands, don't forget that most expressive of all human organs - the face. Raise your eyebrows to express incredulity, frown in disapproval, roll your eyes in astonishment, glare in anger, grimace with pain, but above all, smile! People react positively to a smile, it is an unconscious reflex. Except in the most solemn moments of your closing appeal, always smile. A little girl once told her mother, "I like Pastor Down's sermons because he always smiles."

Particularly when you are telling a story, become an actor. Face right and slump in dejection as you repeat the prodigal son's words, "Father, I have sinned before heaven and in your sight", then straighten up and face left, beaming with joy, as you order the servants, "Quick, bring a robe, ring, sandals, and kill the fatted calf!" Help your audience to live the story with you. Fight with the lion as Samson strangles it, swing the sling as David advances on Goliath, exult with savage joy as the walls of Jericho come tumbling down.

This is particularly important in the children's story. Children have lively imaginations and given a little incitement they will be able to picture the events of your story as you act it out in front of them. A vivid story is far better remembered than a bland, boring one.

Dignity in the pulpit is all very well, but your purpose is not to impress the audience with your dignified mien; your purpose is to communicate the words of God. Isaiah walked naked, Jeremiah hurled pottery, Ezekiel shaved his head and starved himself, all in order to make their messages more impressive to their hearers. If dignity hinders communication, be undignified.

Dress

For greatest effectiveness the minister must not allow anything to distract his hearers from his message. He is merely the voice and his personality is only important insofar as it contributes to the acceptability of his words. One of the surest ways of distracting your audience is by a peculiarity of behaviour or appearance.

I clearly remember a *Week of Prayer* speaker at Avondale College, an older pastor who, so far as I can recall, spoke well and earnestly. Unfortunately he had the unconscious habit of making lengthy pauses during which he lingeringly licked his lips with a long, pink tongue. Half-way through his first sermon no one was thinking of anything else. In the second sermon everyone was counting - the record was 113 times in his fifth sermon - and whatever the good man had to say was entirely lost sight of.

Your clothing should be dignified and conservative and appropriate to your audience. A black suit and tie may be as out of place in a congregation of non-Christian young people as jeans would be in church on Sabbath morning. Generally speaking, in British churches a preacher is expected to wear a suit in a dark colour such as gray, blue, brown or black. The shirt should be white and the tie is best plain and also in a dark colour. Black churches have the same expectations with the exception of the tie, which can be somewhat flamboyant. Shoes should be well polished and either black or brown. Joggers, boots or sandals are a definite no.

The lady preacher should also dress in a conservative fashion. A dress or suit with a skirt that comes well below the knee is preferable to even the most respectable trouser suit. In black churches (and some white ones) a lady should wear a simple head covering in order not to offend those who have strong views on covered heads. Plain, rather than patterned, tights and comfortable shoes complete the ensemble.

Both sexes must avoid anything in the way of personal adornment: beads, ear-rings and make-up for the ladies or an ostentatious watch, tie-pin or cuff-links in the case of men, can distract your hearers from your message or even cause offence with those who take literally the Biblical injunctions concerning such things. Remember that the same passage speaks of "braided hair" which we can take to include any elaborate and expensive coiffuring for either sex.

Some religious traditions use robes and symbols such as crosses embroidered in copes and stoles. Most evangelical Protestant denominations eschew such things as unnecessary display, but even where they are acceptable, they are usually restricted to the official clergy and lay-preachers are expected to dress in ordinary clothes.

Some denominations or congregations are happy with casual dress rather than a suit and tie, but even there neatness and conservatism should be the rule. It may be acceptable to wear jeans, but not jeans that are slashed and ripped! If your congregation allows you to wear a t-shirt, let it be one that is freshly washed and ironed

In view of what we said in the previous chapter about being able to breathe freely, your clothing should not be restricting.

People will feel that you are talking directly to them if you can, from time to time, look at them or, preferably, look them straight in the eye. The preacher should be constantly scanning his audience, turning his head or even his body from side to side in order to include everyone. A quick smile at someone while looking directly into their eyes not only gets a smile in return but ensures that you will have that person's undivided attention for the next five minutes, even if you are being particularly boring!

Finally, keep your language simple. Only posers use long words. If you simply must use a technical term or a foreign word, immediately give its definition. Aim to be understood by the children in your congregation and you will not go far wrong. It is not a sign of either education or wisdom to lard your speech with words or expressions that are incomprehensible to your audience. Particularly beware of the American habit of extending words and, forsaking the simple verb, turning nouns into lengthy verbs. Instead of "burgled", an American will tell you that he has been "burglarised", which then becomes "burglarisation" and so, naturally, to "burglarisationised".

Avoid jargon. Every church has its jargon terms that conjure up a vivid picture for those familiar with them and total bewilderment for those who are not! A Methodist who hears someone say that his heart was "strangely warmed" will immediately think of the conversion of John Wesley while a non-Methodist will wonder what is so significant about being strangely warmed. A Presbyterian will nod in recognition of the phrase "prevenient Grace" while everyone else is wondering whether they heard correctly or whether they need a hearing aid. Some churches refer to themselves as "the Movement", which may conjure up a completely inappropriate picture in the mind of a nurse who has been concerned all night with the bodily functions of her patients. Indeed, some jargon phrases may be offensive: "washed in the blood of the Lamb" or "nailed to a tree" may be meaningful to older Christians but a complete turn-off to non-Christian visitors!

Unless you know that you are talking to a congregation of half-witted militants, avoid "political correctness". It is painful to listen to the laboured, not to say tortured, constructions used by some people in order to avoid saying "he" or "she". Compare:

A woman walks into a shop and says to herself, "I need a new handbag"

with its politically correct version:

A person walks into a shop and says to themself, "I need a new handbag"

Not only is there the contradiction between "person" (singular) and "themself" (neither singular nor plural), but who else but a woman would be wanting a new handbag? All you have achieved is to make yourself look ridiculous. At best you will evoke scorn in any listener with an education, at worst you will provoke murderous rage, but in either case you have lost the opportunity to convey your message in an effective manner.

Reading Scripture

Recently I attended a service in a Church of Scotland church. At the start of the service the minister proclaimed from the back of the church, "Please be upstanding for the Entry of the Bible". Everyone stood as the elder carried a large pulpit Bible down the aisle, followed by the minister. The same ceremony, in reverse, was carried out at the end of the service. In a very dramatic way, this showed the primacy of the Bible in that church.

In most church traditions, every sermon begins with a reading from Scripture. Unless your church follows a set pattern of readings, the passage you choose should be relevant to your topic. It may introduce what you have to say, illustrate it, or provide the basis for your conclusion.

In general, a Scripture reading should be about twelve verses long. Of course, in different situations you may wish to use just a single verse or read a whole chapter, but twelve verses is a good average. It is not so short that you show disrespect to the word of God, nor so long that its point is forgotten by your hearers.

I believe that it is disrespectful to God's word to read it in a sing-song voice as if it were some sort of incantation. (Anglican clergy are particularly prone to this error.) Rather, we should read it with meaning. Nehemiah boasts that at the great festival he organised, "The Levites read from the Book of the Law of God, making it clear and giving the meaning so that the people could understand what was being read." (Nehemiah 8:8)

Reading aloud is a skill that few people possess. It involves either being very familiar with the passage or being able to read ahead of what you are saying aloud, in order to work out what comes next. Listen to some of the dramatic readings from books given over BBC Radio. Notice how the reader's voice changes as he portrays the various characters in the book and reverts to "normal" when he reads the descriptive passages. We should aim to be at least as good when we are reading the most important book in the world.

"Jesus entered Jericho and was passing through. (*pause, then in a 'meanwhile, back on the ranch' type of voice*) A man was there by the name of Zacchaeus: he was a chief tax collector and was (*emphasise*) wealthy. (*back to normal voice*) He wanted to see who Jesus was, but, being a short man, he could not because of the crowd. So, he ran ahead and climbed a sycamore-fig tree to see him, since Jesus was coming that way. When Jesus reached the spot He looked up and said to him, (*commanding tone*) 'Zacchaeus, come down immediately. I must stay at your house today.' (*normal voice*) So he came down at once and welcomed Him gladly. All the people saw this and began to mutter, (*mutter in a complaining voice with emphasis on the last word*) 'He has gone to be the guest of a sinner!' (*normal voice*) But Zacchaeus stood up and said to the Lord, (*stutter slightly with joy and nervousness*) 'L-L-Look, Lord, h-h-ere and n-now I give h-h-alf of my possessions to the poor - and - and - and if I have cheated (*emphasise the any's*) anybody out of anything, I will pay back four times the amount.' (*normal voice*) Jesus said to him, (*sound slightly amused*) 'Today salvation has come to this house, because this man, too, is a son of Abraham.'"

Use every oratorical trick to make the words of Scripture come alive for your hearers. Emphasise important words, slow down or speed up delivery, insert meaningful pauses, shout for joy when it is appropriate and even squeeze out a sob or a tear as Mary exclaims, "Lord, if You had been here, my brother would not have died." Your aim should be to send chills down the hearers' spines so that they are gripped by the passage and cannot resist rushing home to find out what happened next!

I remember Pastor Victor Hall, the college chaplain, taking a series of worships not long after the *New English Bible* first came out. All he did was read the story of David, without comment, a chapter at a time. Partly it was the newness of the modern language presented to an audience used to the archaic *King James Version*, but mainly it was the dramatic way in which Pastor Hall read. Although the story is one of the best known in the Bible, he had us all hanging on his every word and eagerly crowding into Moor Close chapel to hear the next instalment.

To read and communicate the sense of what you are reading, you must pay attention to punctuation. A full-stop (period, for Americans) is the end of the sentence. You not only pause, but you let the tone of your voice drop to indicate that a significant stopping place has been reached. Commas, on the other hand, are the shortest pauses, even though they are often vital to the meaning of the sentence. To quote the title of a popular book, "the panda bear eats shoots and leaves" - but consider the entirely different picture conjured up by "the panda bear eats, shoots, and leaves."

Colons and semi-colons call for pauses longer than the comma but shorter than the full-stop. A question mark will call for your voice to rise interrogatively at the end of the sentence whereas an exclamation mark calls for excitement. By paying attention to punctuation even St Paul's longest and most complex sentences can be rendered intelligible to your listeners.

And don't forget that dashes and brackets should also be marked by variations in your voice as you read what comes between them and then return to the continuation of what came before them.

I'm afraid that when it comes to public reading, there is no modern version which can compete with the *King James Version* – provided it is read with meaning. Compare:

Behold, I show you a mystery; we shall not all sleep, but we shall all be changed.

with

Let me tell you a secret; we won't all sleep, we'll all be changed.

Try reading the whole of that passage – 1 Corinthians 15:51-57 – as dramatically and meaningfully as you can.

(Voice low, resonant and mysterious) Behold, I shew you a mystery; we shall not all sleep, but we shall, all, be changed. *(Faster and dramatically)* In a moment, in the twinkling of an eye, at the last trump: *(let your voice ring triumphantly)* for the trumpet shall sound, and the dead shall be raised incorruptible, *(slowly and emphatically)* and we shall be changed. For this corruptible must put on incorruption, and this mortal must put on immortality. *(Reasonable, stating the obvious)* So when this

corruptible shall have put on incorruption, and this mortal shall have put on immortality, (*emphasise the next word*) then shall be brought to pass the saying that is written, (*emphasise that this is a quote by a change in voice*) Death is swallowed up in victory. (*Dramatically, for you are issuing a challenge!*) O death, where is thy sting? O grave, where is thy victory? (*Quieter, as you explain the problem*) The sting of death is sin; and the strength of sin is the law. (*Once more triumphantly*) But thanks – thanks! – be to God, which giveth us the victory through our Lord Jesus Christ.

I have always aimed to make the word of God sound so exciting and fascinating that people will want to look up the Scripture Reading when they get home, just for the pleasure of reading something so interesting. I like to think, from the comments that people have made to me at various times, that I have not altogether failed in this ambition. I can, therefore, urge you to follow my example in this respect.

Hymns and Benediction

There are two final things I wish to mention: the hymns and the benediction. Well-chosen hymns can add to your message and drive it home to the hearer's heart.

As a general rule your first hymn should be one of praise to God, and these are generally grouped near the front of the hymn book.

Except for special hymn-singing services, most church traditions have three or four hymns in the course of a morning service. If you have children in the congregation, then the second hymn can be a children's hymn – which may or may not be related to your subject. Otherwise, if there are only three hymns, you should pick one that introduces your subject or is in some way related to it.

However if there are four hymns, then the second hymn can be an excellent opportunity to introduce new music to the congregation. Make sure, however, that you have warned the organist or musicians in advance so that he or she is ready to play the new hymn confidently. It also helps if you can lead the singing, otherwise go over the hymn with someone who has a good strong voice, so that he or she can lead the congregation in singing the new hymn.

If there are only three hymns then you have no choice but to introduce new music right before your sermon, but if there are four, then avoid putting the new hymn immediately before the sermon. Instead choose something that is familiar and which prepares the congregation to listen to your message.

It is with the final hymn that you should attempt to reflect your subject. Often the hymn can be an effective way of making an appeal to your congregation. It can send your congregation out into the world whistling or humming its words which, throughout the week will remind them of your message. The final hymn must be a familiar one, lest the congregation be distracted from your message by the work of learning a hymn or worse, by the unpleasant experience of stumbling through an unknown one.

There are two schools of thought regarding the benediction: the first regards it as an opportunity to repeat the main heads of the sermon and hammer home the message under the guise of talking to God. Thinking of the sermon outline given earlier, such a benediction might be something like this:

"Lord, we thank Thee that Jesus is coming back as He has promised, that the signs assure us that His return will be soon. We know that He is coming to save the righteous and judge the wicked and we pray that we might be ready to meet Him when He returns. Amen."

Personally I find something unpleasant in this hectoring of God just in order to reiterate one's sermon. The place for that is in the Conclusion.

I therefore prefer the second school of thought, the priestly. The benediction is the words of blessing spoken by the minister to carry his people through the coming week. The Bible has a number of benedictions, from the priestly blessing "May the Lord lift up His countenance upon you ..." to the conclusions to Paul's letters: "May the grace of our Lord Jesus Christ ..." One of these may be used or adapted or, of course, the minister is free to devise his own. Personally I always say:

"Now may the grace of God, the love of Jesus and the close friendship of the Holy Spirit, be with us all, till He come. Amen."

The preacher's stance when pronouncing the benediction should also be considered. Many in the Protestant tradition give a sort of Nazi salute, raising the right hand and extending it out toward the congregation. Try it in front of a mirror and see how the action rucks up the coat! The double-handed Nazi salute is twice as undignified and unattractive in appearance. In any case, this posture is hardly appropriate to the first type of benediction.

The symbolism of the posture is also questionable. By extending the hand palm-down the minister is, as it were, imparting his own blessing to the congregation. We have no sanctity of our own to give to anyone: we receive from God and pass on to the waiting people that which we have received.

Thus both symbolically and aesthetically, the pose adopted by the early Christians (and by Catholic priests) is to be preferred. Search on the internet for pictures of the "Lullingstone fresco" which depicts early Christians praying. To copy them, stand with your arms by your side then, keeping your upper arm still, raise your forearms up and out with your palms uppermost and slightly angled towards the congregation. Hold your hands at the point where they are about mid-way between shoulder and elbow and pronounce the benediction in that posture. As you say the word "Amen" you may, if you wish, bring your hands together in a way similar to the famous "Praying Hands" picture, hold for a moment or two and then step down from the platform and make your way to the back of the church, ready to say farewell to the departing congregation.

Of course, some traditions call for the priest or minister to make the sign of the cross towards the congregation as the benediction is pronounced. If that is your custom, be sure to practice the action in front of a mirror and while wearing whatever garments are your usual garb. Make sure that you are as impressive and reverent as the sign demands!

The preacher must, at the very least, be on time. I have no patience with those who regard themselves as "stars" and behave like *prima donnas*. I have known some so-called ministers who keep their congregation waiting for five or ten minutes as a matter of course - and then disappear into the vestry at the end of the sermon, ignoring the people of God as they leave the building.

Ideally the preacher should come early. I always try to arrive half an hour before the rest of the congregation. This gives me time to pray and to sit in quietness before God in preparation for the sermon. As I am also the pastor, I then go out and greet the congregation as they come in the door. Even if you are a visiting speaker or a lay preacher you should at least become acquainted with your congregation. People are more willing to listen to someone they know!

Make sure that you greet everyone: there is nothing worse than the preacher who engages in long conversation with a favoured few and ignores everyone else. Even if you have particular friends in the congregation, greet them just as warmly - but no more warmly - than you greet the smallest child or the ragged tramp who wanders in off the street.

When you greet people, smile broadly as if you are delighted to see them and offer them your hand. (The old idea that you wait for a lady to offer her hand is not only not observed these days but, in my opinion, should not apply to ministers. We greet everyone, regardless of age, sex, colour or any other distinction.) Avoid offering a limp hand; there is nothing worse than the "dead fish" kind of handshake. At the same time, be aware that a too firm handshake can actually be painful for someone with arthritis. Try to strike the happy medium!

At the end of your sermon go to the door at the back of the church and bid farewell to the congregation as they file out. They may have questions they wish to ask you; they may have objections they wish to raise; it is even possible that they may wish to congratulate you on the excellence of your sermon!

The Congregational Prayer

In many churches it is the custom for the church elder to give the prayer during the service. If you are a visiting speaker, it is a good idea to offer the local man the opportunity to do so: he knows the people and their needs in a way you do not.

However if you are called upon to offer the main prayer, do give some thought to what you are saying. This is not a time for you to display your eloquence, nor is it the time for some vague but benevolent thoughts. You are the spokesman (or woman) for the congregation, giving voice to their worship and their concerns before God. You are speaking to God on behalf of *everyone* in the congregation, from the youngest child with a birthday to the joyful young couple newly married to the worried man facing redundancy to the old woman concerned about the doctor's appointment next week.

What things are appropriate for all these people? Without being prescriptive, let me share with you the outline I have in mind when I offer the congregational prayer.

> Thanks for physical blessings
> Petitions for the less fortunate
> Petitions for those serving others
>
> Thanks for spiritual blessings
> Petitions for fellow Christians
> Petitions for the unsaved
>
> Prayer for minister and congregation
> Prayer for those absent
> Prayer for the young
> Final petitions

The exact words that are offered will vary from week to week. Under physical blessings you may list food, homes, clothing. In late summer a good harvest deserves mention, in winter warm homes come high up the list!

Then you turn to any events which have hit the headlines in your own community or around the world – wars, natural disasters, crimes or economic problems. If any of these have impacted your congregation, they require special mention. Pray for missionaries and aid workers.

It is well to remind ourselves of the spiritual blessings we enjoy – freedom of conscience, a lovely church, the Bible in our own languages, the salvation Jesus offers, and so on. Advent and Easter call for special mention in this section. Then we remember our fellow Christians, particularly those who are being persecuted. Finally we pray for the heathen generally and more particularly for those for whom we are especially responsible – our friends, neighbours, relatives and fellow citizens.

Finally we turn to ourselves: pray for the preacher and those who listen to him. Pray for those who are absent – and a list of any who are sick should be in your mind or written on a slip of paper in your hand! Pray for young people, who are the future of the church.

Finish the prayer with a dedication of all who are present or with a reminder that Jesus is coming soon or in some other way. Some like to finish by inviting the congregation to join in reciting the *Lord's Prayer*. In larger churches the choir may sing a response.

Sometimes, instead of praying myself, I simply announce the various topics and invite the congregation to silently offer their own prayers.

> First of all we give thanks to God for the physical blessings we have received. (*20 second pause*). Now we think of those less fortunate then ourselves, particularly those affected by the earthquake in .... (*20 second pause – and substitute whatever news item is appropriate*). Let us remember before God those who are working for their fellowmen. (*20 second pause*)
> And so on.

In many churches both congregation and officiant kneel during the congregational prayer, a custom of which I approve. However the culture of your society or the particular circumstances of your church may make this impossible; the congregation remain seated and the officiant stands at the pulpit.

Whether standing or kneeling, hold your head up and speak your prayer with all the volume and clarity of your sermon. God may hear you if you bury your face in your hands and mumble, but how will Brother Jones in the back row know when to say "Amen" if he can't hear and understand what you are saying?

I have seen some places where the person offering the prayer first invites "prayer requests" and the service is held up while a man in the fourth row goes into interminable detail about his neighbour's health and forthcoming operation. Quite apart from the fact that the neighbour might be vastly embarrassed to know that his personal life is being bruited abroad, not every medical problem is suitable for public comment – and meanwhile someone in the back row has an urgent problem but is too shy to speak up in front of the whole church!

A much better method is to have a prayer request book at the back of the church or a form that can be filled out and handed to the deacon or elder before the service. Have the book or the forms in front of you as you pray and mention each request – but Mr Brown's haemorrhoids and Mrs Brown's hysterectomy can be referred to in suitably vague language that is suitable for church and for sparing their blushes.

There is, however, one prayer that the minister will almost certainly be asked to offer and that is the prayer over the offering. As a general – but not invariable – rule, if the deacons use offering bags or boxes, either there is no prayer or the prayer is offered before the collection is made. If the deacons use plates then you will almost certainly be asked to pray.

Leave the pulpit and stand in a suitable position to receive the plates from the hands of the deacons. Accept the plates onto your open hands and then elevate them slightly as you pray. In the old Jewish temple the priests offered "a heave offering" – and when the offering consisted of a sheaf of wheat or an animal, I guess "heave" was probably the *mot juste*! When you have dedicated the offering to God and His service, either return the plates to the deacons or place them on the table before the pulpit.

Seeing as I am already out of the pulpit, this is the point at which I like to give the children's story.

Technology

There are two forms of technology that every preacher will encounter from time to time. The first, and most universal, is the microphone.

Old fashioned preachers prided themselves on never using a microphone; some of them did indeed possess fine, strong voices that could be heard in the largest church or hall. George Whitfield, a contemporary of the Wesleys, could preach in the open air to a congregation of thousands and be heard distinctly by every one of them.

Even if you are blessed with such a voice, there is one good reason why you should use the microphone: the hearing aid loop, which is a method by which those who use hearing aids can hear the preacher's voice undistorted by ambient sounds. Nearly all churches in Western countries now have to fit a loop system by law.

The most common microphone is fixed to a stand on the pulpit, which means that the preacher has to be fixed in position and facing forward. If he turns his head, his voice misses the microphone and there is a loss of volume which renders him inaudible.

The next most common is the hand-held microphone, either wireless or on a lead. Very expensive microphones can cope with the pop star who holds the microphone to his mouth as if he were licking an ice-cream cone, but very few churches can – or if they can, bother to – afford such microphones! The result is that as soon as you say a word beginning with 'p' or 'b', there is a "pop" as your plosive breath hits the microphone. The solution is a windshield - a foam cap on the microphone that smooths out the gusts of breath, or for you to hold the microphone under your chin so that it picks up your voice but plosive gusts of air miss it.

Less common is the lapel microphone or the headset microphone. In the first a small microphone is attached to your tie or lapel; in the second a headset holds a small microphone to one side of your mouth. My favourite is the wireless lapel microphone: it leaves my hands free to gesture or operate equipment, it leaves me free to move about, it picks up my voice whichever way I am facing and even when I turn my head (though I admit that the headset microphone is even better in that respect).

As I cannot rely on every church having a wireless lapel mic, I have my own which I carry around with me, together with a set of adaptors so that it can fit just about any PA system.

The second form of technology is the computer and video projector. Before dismissing this as a gimmick, consider the following: research carried out in the 1970s showed that we remember 10% of what we hear, 20% of what we see, but 60% of what we both see and hear! If you illustrate your sermons, you immediately make them six times more effective.

There are other advantages: these days people bring a variety of Bibles to church with them (if they bring any at all) and while some in your congregation are reading the venerable *King James Version*, others are misleading themselves with that frightful *The Message*! Project your Scripture Reading and other passages from the Bible onto a screen and you ensure that everyone is reading from the same version, even those who didn't bring a Bible to church.

Make sure, however, that you are honest with the word of God. You may be tempted to leave out a word or phrase that is not relevant to your message; if you do, be sure to indicate what you have done with the usual ellipsis - "..." - but it is better still not to leave anything out. After all, if you were reading from the paper Bible, your congregation would be aware of that word or phrase.

I remember a funeral in an Anglican church where the speaker wished to emphasise that the deceased was now in heaven looking down on us all, so when he read from 1 Corinthians 15 he carefully omitted the verses which speak of the change from mortal to immortal taking place at the Second Coming. I also remember a Catholic church at the beginning of Lent where the priest, supposedly reading from the gospels, read that John came preaching "Repent and do penance, for the kingdom of heaven is at hand". (The words "do penance" do not occur in Scripture.) In both cases I was appalled equally at the dishonesty of the preacher and the ignorance of the congregation!

Hymns projected onto a screen give you the freedom to use hymns or extra verses which are not in the church's normal hymn book. In addition, by lifting people's heads to look at the screen instead of peering down at a hymn book, you improve the singing.

Project the heads of your sermon onto a screen and people will remember them better. Use pictures to make your subject come alive and more memorable. Leave the conclusion or appeal of your sermon on screen to impress it on people as the service ends.

The most common display program is Microsoft's *Power Point* or the very similar OpenOffice program *Impression* which has the advantage of being free. Be wary of these programs; they can be time consuming to set up and the temptation to use gimmickry - text that dances onto the screen, fonts surrounded by a pink glow, and similar horrors - can be irresistible. It has become so clichéd that some businesses now ban *Power Point* presentations!

I have written my own software which allows text or pictures to be displayed but also allows me to underline or circle important points or draw lines or arrows linking things. It is simple, but effective (write to me at kkdown@nwtv.co.uk and I'll gladly send you a copy).

Whatever you use, be careful that your colour scheme is both legible and harmonious. Red text on a maroon background is not legible, neither is black text on a dark blue background. White text on a black background is probably easiest on the eye, but I understand that dyslexic people often have trouble reading it. For them bright yellow text on a dark blue background is easiest. For the sake of clarity, use bold text or a bold font. My favourite is "Damaged", but "Ariel Bold" is a good choice.

Shocking pink and violent violet are probably not good colour combinations. If you have a picture background, the choice of text colour can be complicated: you may need white text to stand out against dark trees in the bottom part of your picture but black text to stand out against the light blue sky! My software automatically provides a shadow, which is a good solution to both situations.

Make sure that your text is big enough so that someone at the back of the church can read it. If you have a long quote or Scripture passage, the temptation is to use a smaller font size in order to fit it all in on the screen. It is far better to split the quotation into two or more slides and use a large font size.

The biggest and most annoying fault, however, is the person who has a succession of bullet points on screen and simply reads them to his audience. For pity's sake, the people in the audience can read for themselves! Limit what is on screen to a short, pithy sentence or phrase and then in your speech enlarge and expand on it.

Below in large letters is what you should show on screen. Underneath is a paragraph of italic text, which is what you say. Don't be tempted to put the longer passage on the screen! Notice how the large words are a summary of the point you wish to make, but the words in italics are the full expansion that drives the summary home.

Jesus will come visibly

The Bible tells us that when Jesus comes, every eye will see Him. Jesus uses the illustration of lightning flashing across the sky from east to west to impress on us the fact that everyone will see Him coming. You won't need anyone to tell you that Jesus is on His way: you'll be able to look up and see it for yourself. There will be the sound of a trumpet, the voice of the archangel, the crashing earthquake, the fall of mountains, the roaring of the sea, all will draw our eyes irresistibly to the sky where the Son of Man appears in the clouds of heaven, attended by hosts of angels. Jesus will come visibly!

Remember the old dictum that "one picture is worth a thousand words"; don't just put words - headings and bullet points - on screen. Use pictures as well, but make sure that the pictures do indeed add to your sermon rather than detract from it. Pictures can be in the form of maps, diagrams or charts as well as drawings and photographs. A well-thought out diagram, particularly one which develops as the sermon progresses, can add tremendously to the effectiveness of your sermon.

When thinking of maps, there are the traditional maps with countries and cities labelled neatly, but these can be a distraction. It is hardly relevant to the journeys of Paul to show his itineraries divided between the modern countries of Israel, Cyprus, Syria, Turkey, Greece and Italy, with "Istanbul" in large letters but no mention of Iconium or Derbe! If you don't have a Bible atlas from which you can copy, a useful alternative is to select the relevant area on Google Earth and save it, then draw on it - either in advance or as you talk, if you use my program - the routes followed by the apostle.

Not all of us are artistically gifted and your talents, like mine, may be limited to drawing arrows between boxes or circling important words. Fortunately the internet is a wonderful source of pictures and illustrations. My favourite is www.bing.com/images where you just type in a few key words and, no matter how arcane your subject, something is bound to pop up. (Mind you, sometimes what appears has very little to do with any topic suitable for a sermon and a church audience, but you just have to live with that!)

Be aware, however, that many if not most of the pictures Bing will offer up are little more than thumbnails, perhaps 170x90 pixels in size. Your computer and projector operate at 1024x768 or larger and although most software can scale a small picture up, the results are not always happy. No matter how appropriate a picture may be, if it comes out on the screen as a blurry mess, don't use it.

I am not sure what the position on copyright is, but I feel that anything on the internet which does not have a copyright notice attached is fair game and provided I use the picture for my own purposes and not for making money, then that's ok. If, however, you intend to sell your *Power Point* presentation or broadcast it over television, then you really should get permission from the copyright holder.

If you are worried, then a digital camera is your friend. You can photograph people and things, you can even scrawl your own pictures (or get someone with artistic talent in the church to do it for you) and photograph them. Here, however, you will find the opposite problem of pictures 5000x3500, far larger than you need. They not only take up more space on your hard drive and your memory stick, but they take longer to load and produce a detectable hesitation between one slide and the next. The freeware program *The Gimp* will help you to scale the pictures down to a smaller size.

I scale all my pictures up or down to 1280x840, hoping in this way to make allowance for the higher definition projectors of the future. You may prefer to standardise on a different figure, but do make sure that your pictures are the very best possible. You don't want to distract your audience with the awfulness of your illustrations!

Power Point-style presentations can incorporate sound as well as video and you may wish to include a verse from a hymn or a short clip from YouTube in your sermon. Be careful not to overdo such gimmicks, but at the same time don't rule them out completely.

My program and the OpenOffice version of *Power Point* (*Impression*) allow what is called a "Presenter Screen"; that is, what you see on the screen of your laptop is not the same as what is projected for your audience to see. A typical presenter screen includes a section for notes, a thumbnail of the present picture and the next one, and a clock. Knowing what is coming next can be extremely useful, particularly if the next picture or title is intended to be a dramatic revelation. You don't want to announce some important point only to have the point come up on screen when you have all but finished talking about it!

The usefulness of the clock should be obvious. In fact, my program displays two clocks, one giving the local time and the other the elapsed time since the start of your presentation. The section for notes is somewhat redundant, as the pictures and titles themselves provide all the notes that you need. However there may be details which are not appropriate to put on screen for the audience to see – dates, facts, figures – and these can be in the notes for you to incorporate in your sermon as required.

Creating a good presentation is a skill that not everyone possesses. Try to imagine that you are making a video to show on television: what images will enhance your spoken commentary? Will large screenfulls of text be interesting to your viewers or a turn-off? Can that paragraph be condensed to a single memorable sentence? (You read the paragraph from the presenter screen, but your audience only sees the sentence.) Do the bullet-points follow one another in logical and developing order?

There is, however, one final all-important point: make sure that everything works! I have my own laptop, my own projector and my own extension leads and cables. If there is a computer and projector in the church, I am happy to use theirs (though be aware that not everyone is as careful as you are and I have before now picked up viruses on my memory stick from church computers!) I get to the church at least half an hour before the service begins and check that their equipment works, that my presentation works in their equipment, that they have the fonts I need installed on their computer, and so on. If I use my own equipment, I make sure that it is all set up and operating before the congregation arrives.

Oh, and while you're at it, make sure that you use the keystone correction feature of your projector to ensure that the sides of your picture are perfectly vertical and the top and bottom are perfectly horizontal. The top and bottom are set by placing your projector so that in the horizontal plane it is at exactly 90 degrees to the screen. The sides are set by the keystone correction feature on your projector. Ideally this should be two easily accessible buttons on your projector or its remote control, but some projectors require you to find a menu item. Be confident that you know how to find that menu item before you get to your venue.

There is nothing worse than the minister who turns up just before the sermon and then tries to set up his computer only to find that it doesn't talk to the church's projector or the church's remote control isn't compatible with his laptop or he can't find the keystone memory option in the projector's menu system. Ten minutes after the service should have started, the minister and several helpful deacons are still struggling to get things working! Meanwhile everyone - including the preacher - is getting hot and bothered. and the air of calm and ordered reverence that should prevail is notable by its absence!

Communion

Strictly speaking, the Communion service is not part of preaching; nevertheless, there is usually a sermon in association with the Communion, so it is not entirely irrelevant to include it here. If your denomination celebrates the Eucharist on a weekly basis, then you will need to regard your sermon as separate from the Eucharist, otherwise you will not provide a balanced diet for the flock. Many Protestant churches, however, celebrate the Eucharist or Communion only once a quarter or even less often. In such a case you should seek to make your sermon topical and shorter than usual in order to allow plenty of time for the Communion.

The Communion service is not the time to talk about the Mark of the Beast or the identity of the 144,000. Instead you should focus on the themes of Communion - the meaning and symbolism of the bread and wine, the grace of God in giving His Son to die for us, sin and forgiveness, and so on. If a normal sermon is 25 minutes long, then a Communion sermon should be around 15 minutes long.

If your denomination has a set liturgy for use during Communion then you need read no further, for you will be expected to follow that liturgy. Other Protestant churches do not have a set liturgy and it is up to each celebrant to decide what to do. In such cases most ministers read either the account of the Last Supper in the synoptic gospels or St Paul's advice to the Corinthians in 1 Corinthians 11. Of the two, I prefer the latter, which I regard as the earliest liturgy in the church.

Whichever you use, it is important that the words, "This is My body" and "This is My blood" (or, in 1 Corinthians, "This cup is the new testament in My blood") should be said. Known as the "Words of Institution", they mark out the bread and the wine as something "other", something special. I do not believe in Transubstantiation and even have my doubts about Consubstantiation, but I do firmly believe that when those words are pronounced, that mixture of flour and water you hold becomes something sacred. After all, very few churches will take the consecrated bread and use it with sour cream and chive dip in the after-service pot-luck dinner! Say the words which Jesus Himself said and let

God do what He will with the symbols - and if it should be His will to turn them into the actual body and blood of Christ, then let God be sovereign!

The communion service is all about service, for it remembers Christ's service to us and to His disciples when He washed their feet. (Some churches practise a ceremony of foot-washing before Communion and it can be a very beautiful and meaningful rite.) It is fundamental, therefore, that no person serves himself. The minister hands the plates or trays of bread and wine to the deacons who serve the congregation. The deacons then return to the minister who serves them and then, if the minister is alone, one of the deacons will serve him; if there is a church elder, then the minister and elder serve each other. Under no circumstances should the minister serve himself, as if he were the source of blessing, too grand to be served by anyone else.

Some churches use a single cup and the congregation come to the front to be served by the minister, others prefer hygiene to symbolism and use individual small cups, taken round to the congregation by deacons. Neither is Biblical but neither should be rejected on that grounds, as the Bible does not set out an order of service for any Christian rites.

The tradition with which I am most familiar celebrates Communion once a quarter and uses individual glasses, but the order of service I suggest below can be adapted to any style of service. The only reason I suggest it is because I have seen and experienced some Communion services which were so lacking in order and reverence that they were embarrassing.

This, then, is the order of service I use and recommend.

The congregation is seated, the minister (and elder) sit behind or to either side of the Communion table and the bread and wine are uncovered. The minister or the elder then stands and reads:

For I have received of the Lord that which also I delivered unto you, That the Lord Jesus the same night in which He was betrayed took bread: and when He had given thanks, He brake it.

All then kneel while the minister or one of the deacons prays, giving thanks to God for the body - the Incarnation and the victorious earthly life - of Jesus. When everyone has resumed their seats the minister and the elder together break the bread into thumbnail-size pieces and hand the plates to the deacons, who take them to the congregation. When all have been served the minister stands and reads:

Jesus said, "Take, eat: this is My body, which is broken for you: this do in remembrance of Me".

After a suitable pause for silent prayer and for swallowing the minister or elder then stands and reads:

After the same manner also He took the cup, when He had supped, saying, "This cup is the new testament in My blood."

Again all kneel while the minister or one of the deacons prays, giving thanks to God for the death of Jesus, through which we have hope for eternal life. When everyone has resumed their seats the minister and the elder give the trays of cups to the deacons who take them to the congregation. When all have been served the minister stands and reads:

Jesus said, "This cup is the new testament in My blood; this do ye, as oft as ye drink it, in remembrance of Me."

After a suitable pause the deacons then take the trays and collect the empty cups and the Communion table is covered. Finally the minister stands and reads:

For as often as ye eat this bread, and drink this cup, ye do shew the Lord's death till He come.

Give great emphasis to those last three words, for the Communion is both a memorial and a foreshadowing - a memorial of Jesus' death and a foreshadowing of His return in glory.

While the bread is being distributed the organist should play softly something relevant to the theme of the Incarnation and even a

Christmas carol would not be out of place! During the distribution of the wine a suitable musical offering might be "Amazing Grace" or "When I Survey". While the cups are being collected a triumphant piece such as "Thine be the Glory" is appropriate.

In Conclusion

If God has called you to preach, answer that call. As a faithful workman (or woman) try to do the very best you can and I hope that the tips in this book will help you become a better preacher. However remember that if God has called you, He has a purpose in so doing. He can see that you - not someone else - is the right person to say what He wants to be said in that particular place and on that particular occasion.

Remember that the success of your sermons does not depend on careful study beforehand - though you should certainly do that - nor does it depend on your mastery of oratory and public speaking techniques - though you will naturally wish to use your best ability to make your message acceptable to your hearers. The only secret to success is to have the Spirit of God speaking through you and then you can leave the results to Him.

A young man set out to walk to his church one winter's day in London, but the snow was coming down so heavily that he turned aside into the first church he came to. There were only a few people there and after a while it became apparent that the preacher for the day wasn't going to make it. One of the old men in the congregation - he might have been the elder - stood up and announced a hymn. Then he read something from the Bible. Then he offered up a short and stumbling prayer and finally he attempted to preach. It wasn't very good. It went something like this:

"My Bible verse was 'Look unto Me and be ye saved'. Um. So that's what we have to do. Er. I mean, look to Jesus. Ah. Er. Well, that's what the verse says: 'Look', so - er - that's all we have to do. Look. Um. 'Look unto Me'. That means, look to Jesus. Er."

And so it went on for four or five interminable minutes and then the old man, looking around for inspiration, caught sight of the young stranger and said, "Young man, have you looked to Jesus? Look! Look to Jesus and you will be saved."

It was probably the lousiest sermon ever preached, but that direct question somehow got through to the mind of the young man where the eloquence of famous preachers had failed and that day Charles Haddon Spurgeon gave his heart to Christ and went on to become the "prince of preachers", a man who led thousands to Christ.

How astonished that old man is going to be when, in the kingdom of God, he discovers just what mighty fruit came from his few halting words - and how thankful he is going to be that he did not try to excuse himself with a feeble "but I can't preach", "I haven't prepared", "I'm too shy".

Jesus promised that in the hour of need, "it shall be given you what ye shall speak". That does not mean that we neglect to study and prepare and practise, but it does mean that when you stand up to preach - and no one is more in need than a preacher in the pulpit - God will give you what to say and He takes the responsibility for the success of your poor efforts on His almighty shoulders.

Only eternity will show the results of your inadequate words.

Other Books

Other books by the same author:

The Woman from Banias Publius Cassius Varo is on his way to Palestine in pursuit of a childhood sweetheart whose father had given her to a more worthy suitor, but now that more worthy husband is dead and Publius can't wait to try to rekindle the flame of old romance. The trouble is the Secunda is sick and no one can cure her. Although Publius leaves, discouraged, Secunda finds the answer to her problems through days of painful toil when a Jewish rabbi, who should have scorned her as a woman, a gentile and unclean into the bargain, shows her a surprising degree of compassion - and as an archaeologist, I am still looking for fragments of the homage Secunda paid to her deliverer.

Bought With the Iron Curtain in tatters, Bill Hughes decides that the time is ripe to explore Poland, but not long after he gets there he is offered a girl - for sale, not rent. When he learns that she is English, he decides to buy her to rescue her from the criminals who are holding her - but discovers that her ordeal has made her mute and terrified. Gradually, however, he wins her trust and just when things seem to be heading for the happy ending she is diagnosed with a new and terrifying disease, Acquired Immune Deficiency Syndrome, about which little is known. Can there be a happy ending after all?

Cherie Bonson - Robomate Nick Hawthorne is a stockbroker and futures trader who makes a spectacular "killing" in Martian Zinc by acting on a tip he received from a space pilot. With all that money burning a hole in his pocket, he can well afford to fulfil all his deepest fantasies when he spots Cherie Bonson, the world's sexiest pop star, for sale as a RoboMate. The fact that she has a Real People Personality doesn't faze him in the least - until he gets to grip with Cherie's personality, which, as the salesman pointed out, does not provide uniform satisfaction. Nick is stumped for a solution until he meets a more than usually mad street preacher shouting about changing hearts of stone for hearts of flesh - but it is Pam Henderson, a former girl-friend, who shows him the long-term answer to his problems.

Fuad This is a rip-roaring tale of adventure set in the dying days of the Crusader kingdom of Jerusalem. A chance encounter on the road to Jericho results in Fuad, a beduin shepherd boy, becoming squire to Sir Guy d'Orleans. He takes up residence in Jerusalem where he gradually learns that Sir Guy is a most unusual Frank, one who works for peace but who runs an extensive network of spies and informers with tentacles in the Sultan's palace in

Damascus and down into Egypt. Sir Guy also has a daughter, a red-haired, green-eyed girl that Fuad first mistook for a djinna, a female djinn. Fuad is sent on various missions for Sir Guy that take him as far afield as Mecca and repeatedly to Kerak, where he meets the fearsome ogre, Reynauld of Chatillon. Finally he is an observer at the disastrous battle of the Horns of Hattin - but what happens after that you will have to buy the book to find out!

The Privatised Community Service Girl The year is 2051 and Britain has turned its back on the liberalism that turned prisons into luxury hotels and cared more for the criminal than for his victim. Steve Russell finds a job as trainer, fitting offenders for their time as "slaves" on the Privatised Community Service scheme. He does his job efficiently and seems set for a dull climb up the career ladder until he meets a girl who believes that slaves should be content in whatever circumstances they find themselves and should serve their owners diligently and faithfully. When he discovers that Jeff, the detestable prison guard, is eager to rape the girl, he impulsively takes her home on Form 407 for extended training and from there one thing leads to another until - well, until Steve's life is turned upside down in ways he could never have expected.

Capelburgh vol 1: Lord of Capelburgh In the first volume of George Crandall's memoirs, he describes how he drew on his engineering background to work out how to travel safely back to the Fourteenth Century to fulfil the requirements of his history degree course. His plan was to live quietly in London and observe the social effects of the Black Death; instead he finds himself appointed by the king as lord of the castle of Capelburgh, a minor fortress way out in the sticks in the north of England. There he meets a cast of mediaeval characters - a priest and his mistress, a voluptuous red-haired Scottish witch, and above all Margaret, the dark-haired, pock-marked daughter of the previous lord who died a traitor's death.

Capelburgh vol 2: Neville's Cross As Lord of Capelburgh George Crandall has feudal responsibilities and the threat of Scottish invasion leads him to bend his mind to the problem of how to keep his people safe if the worst should come to the worst. And when the worst does happen and the feudal host is called out, the feudal levy from Capelburgh stands out among the others for its well-ordered provision and innovative weapons. Then, when battle is joined, George's theories are put to the test against a horde of ravenning Scotsmen armed with fifteen-foot pikes ...

Capelburgh vol 3: The Black Death George Crandall intended to watch the Black Death dispassionately, but as lord of Capelburgh with responsibility for his people, he realises that he can't just sit back and watch half of them die. Drastic public health measures, rigorous quarantine, and a firm line with the many strange characters who visit Capelburgh, all aim at keeping Capelburgh safe - and they might have succeeded if Capelburgh had not been cursed with a stubborn priest who insisted on doing his duty, no matter what the cost.

Capelburgh vol 4: Crisis in Capelburgh Although Capelburgh came through the Black Death almost unscathed, society at large began to break down. Half Capelburgh's villeins leave for the higher wages on offer in the big city and when a band of runaway villeins attacks, the result is a massacre - though thanks to Twenty-second Century technology, it is the invaders who suffer most. Even better, the survivors look likely to make up the numbers in Capelburgh and bring its untended fields back into cultivation. But just as things seem to be looking up another crisis erupts, totally unexpected, and George Crandall and his family have to start packing.

Capelburgh vol 5: Capelburgh Revixit With Capelburgh's population back to pre-plague levels, it is time for newcomers and old villeins to work together - and under George Crandall's leadership the village begins a long, slow climb back to prosperity. The even tenor of village life is disturbed by the arrival of a black woman and her daughter, survivors of a shipwreck off the cliffs of Capelburgh. Even more upsetting is the appearance of Professor Thoroughgood, Crandall's old teacher, from Twenty-second Century Lancaster, who returns to his own time with an unexpected wife. Meanwhile Capelburgh is being turned into a money economy, with both good and bad results.

Capelburgh vol 6: Knight of Capelburgh Life in Capelburgh continues its peaceful course of birth, death and marriage and with problems for George Crandall to solve, such as the homosexual tax assessor, the manic pilgrim, the skryer who seeks to debauch an innocent maid and the man who needed to be hung but didn't deserve it. Into this placid world comes unexpected trouble when the Scots capture Berwick and King Edward himself comes to drive them out and then carry fire and sword throughout Lothian. Unwillingly dragged into the war, George Crandall tries to be as merciful as possible, though his ingenuity is taxed to the utmost when he is ordered to hang Lady Avicia. And, of course, there is the small matter of large-scale arson in Edinburgh!

Capelburgh vol 7: Death in Capelburgh There may be official peace between Scotland and England, but lawlessness still reigns in the Debatable Lands along the border. As Lord of Capelburgh, George Crandall finds himself reluctantly drawn into executing judgement on robbers, fraudsters, and noble murderers. In the midst of it all he can't resist planting the idea for an epic poem in the mind of a talented author, the young Geoffrey Shoemaker. Alas, his successes bring him to the attention of authority and George and his son Ranulf are summoned to take part in King Edward's wars.

Capelburgh vol 8: Seigneur de Chapellebourg The year of Our Lord 1359 brings George Crandall into closer contact with the neighbour Bamburgh castle when Makeda, the part-Ethiopian girl to whom his son Ranulf was committed, was involved in a riding accident. Other significant events of that year included the Translation of the dying breath of St Stephen into its new reliquary and the marriages of both Pippa and Ranulf. However George Crandall is summoned down to London to take part in the climactic invasion of France that will finally give King Edward III the crown of that unhappy country. Meanwhile there are comings and goings between the Fourteenth and the Twenty-second centuries and George has an unlikely companion for his foray into France.

Capelburgh vol 9: The Fall of Capelburgh When the Black Death returns to England for the second time George Crandall is ready to stand another siege - but fate conspires that he ends up in Newcastle as the plague reaches that city. With mounting horror he sees the death toll rise and gladly takes to the sea to escape - only to discover that plague is a shipmate! Just when he thinks that things are finally settling down again, nature strikes a deadly blow at Capelburgh and George and his household are lucky to escape with their lives - but the castle will never recover.

Capelburgh vol 10: Farewell to Capelburgh A wandering minstrel disrupts George Crandall's plans for burial in the Fourteenth Century with an effigy on his tomb. Instead he has to wander around Mediaeval England and then return to the near mythical world of Lancaster, this time taking his beloved wife, Margaret, with him. Even then things do not go smoothly and there are pirates to be encountered, the fear-inducing black robes to be evaded, and heart-breaking tragedy before George comes to his final peaceful haven.

Betty's Scheme Jonathon Appleton is on the trip of a lifetime around the good ole' US of A, partly to mark his early retirement and partly to try and forget the tragic death of his wife. Making an unplanned stop at a small town in rural America, he meets Rosie, a baby with the most beautiful corn-flower blue eyes and her young mother, who is destitute and desperate. He can't let Rosie starve and so he buys her a meal and offers her mother a lift to the nearest big city where she can make a new start - only somehow, things don't work out like that. The miles pass and so do the days and Jonathon falls more and more deeply in love with Rosie until finally, to keep from being parted from her, he opts for a Las Vegas wedding - but will he choose the one in the vampire crypt or the one in the Beunos Aires bordello? And how will he get on with his new father-in-law, who packs a gun and is as mean as a rattlesnake?

The Girl Who Gave Her Body Away The Rev Alexander Hughes has never found time for love and he certainly wasn't expecting cupid to strike when fate led him to a girl in the act of throwing herself over Niagara Falls. Desperate to try and stop her killing herself, he blurts out the first idea that comes into his mind - would she let him have her body if he will promise to kill her mind? Intrigued, the girl agrees - with reservations - and those reservations lead to an in-depth exploration of what it means to be human. That all takes time - and time leads to an all-too-human reaction between the reverend and his temporary house guest, but there is a mystery about the girl, tied up somehow with missing university student Barbara Leeson.

Pascal's Wager The French polymath Blaise Pascal rigorously examined all the "proofs" for God and concluded that they didn't add up. Instead he used his expertise in the field of gambling to come up with a wager: if God does not exist you have nothing to lose by rejecting Christianity, but if God does exist, the penalty for making the wrong choice is pretty devastating. It makes sense, therefore, to bet on the side of God! It seemed an unanswerable argument until people realised that there are many religions and many gods - and the problem of which to pick made the odds incalculable. Or does it? Author Ken Down puts his cynic's hat on and examines the question.

Jumi and the Black Goddess When John Curtis sees a beautiful Indian girl, as pretty as a butterfly in her colourful sari, walking past, his thoughts to turn to love and fortunately the Ram Das Marriage Bureau is at hand to set him up with a suitable girl, Jumeela Gopal, divorced by her previous husband for fear that she has the evil eye. Although of no particular religion himself - Church of England on his passport application form - John is shocked to find his new bride worshipping Kali, the black goddess of destruction. Still, in these culturally sensitive times, John does his best to encourage her not to get involved in a Christian church and finally takes her out to India - and that is where the dark tentacles of heathenism reach out and snare his beloved Jumi.

The Wrong Paul Personal tragedy leaves Charles eager to get away from it all and start a new life and when it turns out that he is the doppelganger for newly-bereaved Linda's husband Paul, it is all too tempting to step into the dead man's shoes. At first all seems to go well, but living a lie leads Charles to forget some of the most important moral principles and it takes a wise old woman with some quirky ideas to get all their lives back on track.

The Lonely Planet A dull news day sets an investigative journalist off on a hunt for something interesting to write about - and what he discovers is the intriguing mystery of George Moreton, who disappeared over half a century before on a routine trip from Heston Flight Centre to Norton airbase. After a bit of poking around he discovers Mr Moreton's own account of the events leading up to the disappearance - an earth-like planet six light years away, two thousand years behind, and a beautiful olive-skinned girl who is to be sacrificed to whatever gods are worshipped by the men who destroyed the Ninth Legion.

Henry Crane's Robots Henry Crane needs additional finance to bring his robots to market and to persuade Sir Geoffrey Barnett to invest, he tells him about the trials and tribulations of developing real personalities in his Robotic Personal Assistants, personalities that will keep the robots caring and honest no matter what temptations come their way. Simple programming would turn out - well - robots; what Henry needs is real artificial people and the only way to achieve that is to set up an artificial world and weed out the good from the bad - but at what cost to Henry and his family?

How to Preach As a popular preacher himself, Ken Down is ideally placed to offer advice on topics as diverse as how to write notes, where to find sermon illustrations, how to use modern media to enhance a sermon, and how to lead a communion service. Whether you are a beginner fresh out of college or an old hand on the downward slope to retirement (though true preachers never retire!) whether you are a lay preacher or an ordained clergyman, there is something here for you.

Daniel: Hostage in Babylon The Biblical book of Daniel has fascinated generations of Biblical scholars and preachers, but now archaeology brings us new information which enables us to recreate the background to the stories that make up the first half of the book. Recent historical studies also aid us in understanding the prophecies of the second half of Daniel. If you have ever been puzzled by the beasts and images, the bloodless hands and the den of lions, this book will unravel the mysteries in a fresh way. The author combines his skills as preacher, archaeologist and historian to make the book of Daniel come alive. (This book is also available in paperback from Amazon.)

Bethlehem Love Story When two refugees turn up in Bronze Age Bethlehem they find a rural society governed by rules that are totally different from those of the surrounding nations. For the younger woman in particular, all is new and strange, but she has little time to marvel for there is food to be gathered and a rich, handsome man who seems to find her attractive. Can the wiles of her mother-in-law bring about the happy ending or is she doomed to a lifetime of poverty and want?

The Resurrection of Sir Ralph Gifford It takes Sir Ralph a few moments of thought to realise that the reason why he is standing in church in his nightgown is that he has been resurrected. His first impression is that he is a ghost, but an encounter with a very solid oaken door disabuses him of that conceit. An eventful, week-long journey to heaven brings more surprises, not all of them welcome - for example, the fact that his beloved Bess is not among the saved. Indignantly he confronts Jesus and insists that there must be some mistake. To his relief, Jesus promises to review Bess's life with him and to abide by his decision. With eager anticipation Sir Ralph enters the Hall of Records, determined to prove God wrong.

Two's Tale You might have thought that there was nothing new to be said about the gospel story, but wait until you hear it from the point of view of No. 2 in the Headquarters Brigade, Palestine Section. The trials and tribulations of trying to run an efficient operation with too few resources, ever increasing demands from management, and an unprecedented emergency situation with not one messiah but two to deal with, gives you a certain sympathy with our hero's belief that it's a devil of a job being a demon!

Made in the USA
Las Vegas, NV
22 December 2021